Zoyka's Apartment
(Zoykina Kvartyra)

The uncomfortable squeeze on early-Soviet housing and citizenry has left us with at least two satiric testimonials—Kataev's *Squaring the Circle,* and Bulgakov's riotous *Zoya's Apartment*—and both are notable for what they had to suppress and for what they were able to get away with. And what Bulgakov, one of the Soviet's greatest counter-voices, got away with in *Zoya's Apartment* is hilarious. That voice is beautifully intact in Saunders' and Dwyer's seamless joining of the play's two original Russian versions, and in their wonderfully speakable and playable English translation. There's a special bonus in this edition: Frank Dwyer's generous Afterword on Bulgakov's life and play illuminates our perception of the mordancy and nuttiness of life in Moscow's schizophrenic Twenties.

—*Leon Katz*

Smith and Kraus *Books For Actors*

GREAT TRANSLATION FOR ACTORS SERIES

Mercadet by Honoré de Balzac, tr. by Robert Cornthwaite

Zoyka's Apartment by Mikhail Bulgakov, tr. by N. Saunders & F. Dwyer

The Sea Gull by Anton Chekhov, tr. by N. Saunders & F. Dwyer

Three Sisters by Anton Chekhov, tr. by Lanford Wilson

The Wood Demon by Anton Chekhov, tr. by N. Saunders & F. Dwyer

The Coffee Shop by Carlo Goldoni, tr. by Robert Cornthwaite

Villeggiatura: The Trilogy by Carlo Goldoni, tr. by Robert Cornthwaite

The Summer People by Maxim Gorky, tr. by N. Saunders & F. Dwyer

Ibsen: 4 Major Plays, tr. by R. Davis & B. Johnston

Ibsen Volume II: 4 Plays, tr. by Brian Johnston

Spite for Spite by Agustin Moreto, tr. by Dakin Matthews

Cyrano de Bergerac by Edmond Rostand, tr. by Charles Marowitz

A Glass of Water by Eugene Scribe, tr. by Robert Cornthwaite

If you require pre-publication information about upcoming Smith and Kraus books, you may receive our semi-annual catalogue, free of charge, by sending your name and address to *Smith and Kraus Catalogue, P.O. Box 127, One Main Street, Lyme, NH 03768. Or call us at (800) 895-4331, fax (603) 795-4427.*

Zoyka's Apartment

A Tragic Farce in Three Acts
by Mikhail Bulgakov

Translated and Adapted by
Nicholas Saunders and Frank Dwyer

A Smith and Kraus Book

A Smith and Kraus Book
Published by Smith and Kraus, Inc.

Manufactured in the United States of America
Cover and Text Design by Julia Hill
Cover artwork by Aline Ordman

First Edition: June 1996
10 9 8 7 6 5 4 3 2 1

Library of Congress Cataloguing-in-Publication Data

Bulgakov, Mikhail Afanas'evich, 1891-1940.
[Zoikina kvartira. English]
Zoyka's Apartment ; a tragic farce in three acts / by Mikhail Bulgakov ;
translated and adapted by Nicholas Saunders and Frank Dwyer. -- Rev. ed.
p. cm. -- (Great translations for actors series)
ISBN 1-880399-93-8
I. Saunders, Nicholas. II. Dwyer, Frank. III. Title. IV. Series.
PG3476.B78Z3513   1995
891.72'42--dc20   95-45899
CIP

Contents

For Gedda and Mary

❧

CHARACTERS

ZOYA DENISOVNA PELTZ (Zoyka, Zoyechka), a widow, 35

MANYUSHKA (Marya Garbatova; Manyushechka, Manyusha), her maid, 22

ANISIM ZOTIKOVICH ALILUYA (Aliluychik), Chairman of the Number 10 Sadovaya Street Apartment House Committee, 42

PAVEL FYODOROVICH ABOLYANINOV (Pavlik, Pavlusha, Pavlushka), 35

GAN–TSA–LIN ("Gasoline"), Chinese, 40

CHERUBIM (Tsen–Tsin–Poh; Cherubimchik, Cherubimka), Chinese, 28

ALEKSANDER TARASOVICH AMETISTOV (Sashka), 38

THE CUTTER (female)

THE SEAMSTRESS (Varvara Nikanorovna)

FIRST LADY, unimportant

SECOND LADY, unimportant

THIRD LADY, unimportant

AGNESSA FERAPONTOVNA, very important

ALLA VADIMOVNA (Allachka), 25

MYMRA (Marya Nikiforovna), 35

LIZANKA (Liza), 23 years old

MADAME IVANOVA, 30

*BORIS SEMYONOVICH GOOS–REMONTNY, Coordinating Director of the Essential Metals Industries *Goos–Remontny means "reconditioned goose."*

TUBBY

VANYICHKA (Vanya)

COMRADE PESTRUKHIN

THE POET

MR. ROBBER, defense attorney

THE SMOKER

THE FOXTROTTER

THE STIFF (Ivan Vassilyevich)

TWO JOB APPLICANTS, female (offstage)

VOICE, (offstage, at Headquarters)

SETTING AND TIME

Moscow, in the 20s of the 20th Century.

Zoyka's Apartment

ACT I

SCENE ONE
The Apartment

A large apartment on the fifth floor of a huge apartment building: Zoyka's living room, bedroom, and hallway. A May sunset blazes through the windows, which look down on a large, noisy courtyard. The windows are open and the sounds that float in seem to emanate from some sort of infernal music box.

A gramophone recording of Chaliapin in an aria from "Faust" floats in and out on waves of various shouting voices:

> *Chaliapin: "On this earth, behold—mankind!"*
> *Voice: "Stoves! We buy stoves!"*
> *Chaliapin: "...bows before one sacred idol..."*
> *Voice: "Knives sharpened! Scissors and knives!"*
> *Voice: "Samovars soldered!"*
> *Chaliapin: "...with great passion and emotion/ Worship idols made of gold..."*
> *Voice: "Moscow Evening News! Get your paper here!"*

Trolleys clang, horns honk. A diabolical symphony. As it subsides, we hear an accordion playing a merry polka. In her bedroom, Zoya changes clothes in front of the mirrored doors of a large wardrobe.)

ZOYA: *(Singing along.)*
    "Come and polka, my sweet angel,
        Oh, my angel, dance with me!…"
    I got it! My permit! I got it!

MANYUSHKA: *(Rushing in.)* Zoya Denisovna! It's Aliluya!

ZOYA: *(Whispering.)* No, no! Tell him I'm not home!

MANYUSHKA: He's already here, the little sneak! He came up the back way…

ZOYA: Well, get rid of him! Tell him I'm gone! *(She hides in the wardrobe.)*

ALILUYA: *(Bursting into the bedroom.)* Anybody home? Zoya Denisovna…?

MANYUSHKA: She's out, I told you! You've got some nerve, barging into a lady's bedroom!

ALILUYA: A lady's bedroom! Under the Soviet System, bedrooms are not permitted. Maybe you'd like one, yourself? …When will she be back?

MANYUSHKA: How should I know? She doesn't report to me.

ALILUYA: She's out with her loverboy, I suppose.

MANYUSHKA: What a crude thing to say, Comrade Aliluya! Just who are you referring to?

ALILUYA: And just who are you trying to kid? Oh, come on, Marya, there are no secrets from the Apartment House Committee. We're always on duty! While one eye sleeps, the other watches. That's what we're here for...So...we're all by ourselves now, huh?

MANYUSHKA: Get out of here, Anisim Zotikovich. You have no business in this bedroom.

ALILUYA: Who do you think you're talking to? Don't you see my briefcase? I'm an official! All doors open before me! Who can say no to me?

(Aliluya attempts to embrace Manyushka.)

MANYUSHKA: Just wait till your wife hears about this! She'll scratch your official eyes out.

ALILUYA: Whoa, stand still! You're spinning like a top!

ZOYA: *(From inside the wardrobe.)* Aliluya, you're a pig!

MANYUSHKA: Oh! *(She runs off.)*

ZOYA: *(Emerging.)* And what a fine Apartment House Committee chairman you are! Very impressive!

ALILUYA: But she told me...I thought...so you're home, then! Why did she lie to me? Oh, what a sly one you are, Zoya Denisovna! You always have something to say...

ZOYA: And if I didn't, Aliluya, you'd eat me up alive. You say such disgusting things. Who exactly is my "loverboy?" Surely you don't mean Pavel Fyodorovich...?

ALILUYA: Oh, what do I know, I'm a simple fellow, I didn't get much education...

ZOYA: Too bad. Look, Aliluya, I'm not even dressed, and you won't get out of my bedroom. Besides, I'm not here.

ALILUYA: What do you mean "not here?" That's a strange thing to say...

ZOYA: What do you want, anyway?

ALILUYA: I've come to make a cubic estimate.

ZOYA: Of Manyushka?

ALILUYA: *(Chuckling.)* The things you say! Whatever pops into your head...

ZOYA: Don't tell me it's another space reduction!

ALILUYA: And why not! You're all by yourself, and you have six rooms.

ZOYA: All by myself? What about Manyushka?

ALILUYA: Manyushka is a maid. She has her allocation. Seven point four cubic yards, off the kitchen.

ZOYA: Manyushka!

MANYUSHKA: *(Coming in.)* Yes, Zoya Denisovna?

ZOYA: Who are you?

MANYUSHKA: I'm your niece, Zoya Denisovna.

ALILUYA: Niece? Heh, heh. That's a good one. The niece who brings in the samovar.

ACT I

ZOYA: Don't be silly, Aliluya. Is there any law against nieces bringing in samovars?

ALILUYA: Where do you sleep?

MANYUSHKA: In the living room.

ALILUYA: Answer me quickly... *(Speaking very fast.)*... What does she pay you?

MANYUSHKA: *(Very fast.)* Not a single kopeck!

ALILUYA: *(Suspiciously.)* And what do you call Zoya Denisovna?

MANYUSHKA: Auntie Zoya!

ALILUYA: Terrible girl!

MANYUSHKA: May I go now, Zoya Denisovna?

ZOYA: *(Laughing.)* You may go, Manyushka, my dear.

(Manyushka darts off, giggling.)

And bring in the samovar. Nobody can forbid it.

ALILUYA: Shame on you, Zoya Denisovna. What a fairy tale! If she's your niece, I'm your aunt.

ZOYA: You're a boor, Aliluya!

ALILUYA: The room in front is also unoccupied!

ZOYA: Only temporarily. The man who lives there is away...on official business.

A: What are you telling me, Zoya Denisovna? He doesn't even ive in Moscow any more! Let's be frank: he slipped you some money from the State Porcelain Bureau and vanished! He's been gone a year. He's a mythical being! And thanks to you and this apartment of yours, I got such a reception at the last Apartment House Committee meeting that I barely escaped with my life. All those old babas were screaming at me: "You're protecting her!" "She must be bribing you!"…Well, that's what they're saying…And don't forget, I'm up for reelection.

ZOYA: Those thieves, what is it they want?

ALILUYA: Just who do you mean by "thieves?"

ZOYA: Your precious committee, of course.

ALILUYA: Those are dangerous words, Zoya Denisovna. Anyone else in my position…

ZOYA: There is nobody else in your position, Aliluya, I'm stuck with you.

ALILUYA: They have passed a resolution to consolidate your space. Half of them were shouting, "Throw her out, throw her out!"

ZOYA: Throw me out? *(She makes the sign of the "fig," a closed fist with the thumb protruding between the second and third fingers.)*

ALILUYA: And how am I to interpret that?

ZOYA: *(Repeating the gesture.)* It's self-explanatory.

ALILUYA: All right, that's it! If I don't allocate at least one room in this apartment to some deserving worker by sundown tomorrow, may I die like a dog! You can give him the fig and see what happens…My deepest respects…*(He starts to go.)*

6

ZOYA: Aliluya! Aliluychik! Just answer me one tiny question. How is it that in such a model building, a true community of comrades, *Monsieur* Goos-Remontny has taken over seven rooms on the first floor?

ALILUYA: I beg your pardon, Zoya Denisovna! Goos has been given a special dispensation for that apartment, since he pays for all our heat.

ZOYA: Nothing personal, Aliluya, but how did Goos manage to get that apartment, ahead of Firsov? How much did he slip you?

ALILUYA: That's enough now, Zoya Denisovna, be careful! I'm a very important person! Goos never gave me a kopeck.

ZOYA: *(In a whisper.)* In the inside pocket of your vest there are some ten-ruble notes. Series MB-1922, numbers 425900 to 425949. Take a look.

(Aliluya unbuttons his vest, takes out a bill, checks the number, and looks up astonished.)

Abracadabra!

ALILUYA: I knew it, Zoya Denisovna! You're in league with the devil! You're a socially dangerous element!

ZOYA: Only to those who are socially dangerous to me. *(Pause.)* So...both Manyushka and my mythical being will keep their rooms?

ALILUYA: Be reasonable, Zoya Denisovna. Not Manyushka. Everybody knows she's a maid.

ZOYA: All right, then. We'll take in one more person.

ALILUYA: What about all your other rooms?

ZOYA: *(Taking out her permit.)* Here.

ALILUYA: *(Reading.)* "This document certifies that Comrade Peltz, Zoya Denisovna, is hereby permitted to open and operate a needlecraft school and workshop"…oh!…"for the wives of workers, for the purpose of making work clothes…additional area is granted…" Well, I'll be damned! Did Goos give you this?

ZOYA: What difference does that make?

ALILUYA: You may only be a woman, Zoya Denisovna, but you're a genius.

ZOYA: A genius! In the last five years, they've stripped me naked, and now I'm a genius! Do you remember how I lived before the revolution?

ALILUYA: Indeed, I do!…But are you really going to open a needle-craft workshop?

ZOYA: Why not? Look at me…I'm walking around in mended stockings. I, Zoya Peltz! Before this regime of yours, I never wore mended stockings. I never wore the same pair twice.

ALILUYA: What a leg…

ZOYA: It's a leg, Aliluya. You never stop, do you? Listen, respected chairman, show my permit to your gang of thieves, and that's it. From now on, as far as they're concerned, Zoya Peltz is dead!

ALILUYA: Yes, a document like this certainly makes everything a little easier. Well, that's a relief!

ACT I

ZOYA: Oh, by the way, I was shopping at Myura's today and they gave me this in change, a fifty-ruble note. I think it's counterfeit. Take a look, you're the expert on banknotes.

ALILUYA: *(Plaintively.)* Zoya Denisovna! *(He looks at the bill.)* It looks all right to me.

ZOYA: And I say it's counterfeit. Take the filthy thing and dispose of it.

ALILUYA: I'll dispose of it. *(He tosses the banknote into his briefcase.)* And maybe we can do something about Manyushka, too.

ZOYA: Good for you, Aliluya, I'm proud of you. As a reward, you may kiss me here, on the mended place...Close your eyes and pretend it's Manyushka.

ALILUYA: Oh, Zoya Denisovna, you're so...

ZOYA: What?

ALILUYA: ...bewitching...

ZOYA: That's enough now. Get out of here. Go on, good-bye. I have to get dressed. Go, go!

(In the distance, a piano plays a bravura passage of Liszt's "Rhapsody #2.")

ALILUYA: Bye. But you've got to tell me today who's moving in. I'll be back. *(He walks toward the door.)*

ZOYA: All right.

(The Liszt stops abruptly, and the pianist begins to play a song. A delicate voice sings Rachmaninoff's setting of Pushkin's poem:

"Don't sing to me, my beauty, do not sing,
The sad and lonely songs, the songs of Georgia...")

ALILUYA: *(At the door; dejected, in a subdued voice.)* Oh, I get it... Before Goos hands out banknotes, he records the numbers... Right?

ZOYA: Brilliant.

ALILUYA: *(Leaving.)* What is the world coming to?

(Aliluya goes out through the living room, just as Abolyaninov hurries in. He looks terrible.)

ABOLYANINOV: Zoyka! May I come in? *(He throws down his hat and cane.)*

ZOYA: Pavlik! Of course, come in. *(In desperation.)* What's wrong, Pavlik? Not again?

ABOLYANINOV: Zoya, Zoya, Zoyka! *(He wrings his hands.)*

ZOYA: Lie down, Pavlik, lie down. I'll get the valerian drops. Would you like some wine?

ABOLYANINOV: Wine and valerian drops!

(The singing continues:
"They remind me of another life,
They remind me of a distant shore...")

Do you really think that's what I need? Valerian drops?

ZOYA: *(Sadly.)* Oh, my God! Then how can I help you?

ABOLYANINOV: Kill me!

ZOYA: Oh, Pavlik! I don't have the strength to watch you suffer! Shall we send to the pharmacy? Do you have a prescription?

ABOLYANINOV: No! That useless doctor of mine is at his dacha. At his dacha! People are dying, and he runs off to his dacha. Get the Chinaman...I can't stand it any longer...the Chinaman!

ZOYA: Yes...all right... *(Calling.)* Manyushka! Manyushka!

(Manyushka appears.)

Pavel Fyodorovich is not well...Run to Gasoline's and pick up his medicine.

ABOLYANINOV: No, Zoya Denisovna! He must come and prepare it here, where I can watch him. He's a thief. As a matter of fact, there's not an honest man left in Moscow...They're all thieves. You can't trust anyone. And that voice keeps torturing me, torturing me: "They remind me...of another life...a distant shore..."

ZOYA: Bring him right away. Get a cab.

MANYUSHKA: What if he's not there?

ABOLYANINOV: Not there? But he has to be there! He has to be!

ZOYA: Find him! Wherever he is, find him! Run! Fly!

MANYUSHKA: I will. *(She runs out.)*

ZOYA: Pavlik, my darling, hold on, be strong. She'll bring him right away.

(Offstage, we hear the Rachmaninoff: "They remind me...")

ABOLYANINOV: "They remind me...of another life." This is such a terrible place, Zoya. My God, these people are so noisy! And the sunset, the sunset on Sadovaya Street is so disgusting. An obscene sunset. Shut the blinds! Shut them, shut them!

ZOYA: I will, I will!

(Zoya draws the blinds. Darkness. Zoyka's apartment disappears.)

Scene Two
A Chinese Laundry

(A wretched basement room lit by a small kerosene lamp. Clotheslines hung with laundry. A sign reading "The Happy Hoswife—Shanghai Landry." Gan-Tsa-Lin stands over an alcohol burner, quarreling with Cherubim.)

GAN-TSA-LIN: Chinese bandit! You crook! You steal silk jacket, you steal cocaine! Where you go so long time? How can believe you?

CHERUBIM: Sh...shh...shut up! You bandit, you!

GAN-TSA-LIN: Get out my laundry, you bandit, you Moscow criminal!

CHERUBIM: What? What? Kick out poor Chinaman? Some bandit take jacket, take way from me! On Svetnoy Boulevar! Some bandit steal cocaine, try kill me, look, look!

(Cherubim shows Gan-Tsa-Lin a scar on his hand.)

I work and work for you, now kick me out? Where get food, one poor Chinaman in Moscow? You no good comrade! Should be kill.

GAN-TSA-LIN: You shut up! You kill me, police get you. Ohh! Communist police! You wait see!

(Pause.)

CHERUBIM: What you say? Kick out assistant? Good! Go hang myself you front gate!

(Pause.)

GAN-TSA-LIN: No more steal? No more rob?

CHERUBIM: No more, no more!

GAN-TSA-LIN: Say, swear to God.

CHERUBIM: Swear to God!

GAN-TSA-LIN: One more time, say, swear to God!

CHERUBIM: Swear to God, swear, swear, swear!

GAN-TSA-LIN: Put on apron! Get to work!

CHERUBIM: Hungry. No food two days. Need bread!

GAN-TSA-LIN: On stove. Take. *(A knock.)* Who, who, who?

MANYUSHKA: *(From outside.)* It's me, Gasoline! Open up.

GAN-TSA-LIN: Aaah, Manooska! *(He opens door.)*

MANYUSHKA: *(Coming in.)* Why do you have your door locked? Some laundry! Always closed!

GAN-TSA-LIN: Ah, Manooska, hello, hello!

MANYUSHKA: Oh, what a pretty face, like an angel! Who's this?

GAN-TSA-LIN: He assistant.

MANYUSHKA: Assistant? Well, well! All right, Gasoline. I need some medicine.

GAN-TSA-LIN: What? Aboyan sick again?

MANYUSHKA: You said it!

GAN-TSA-LIN: Five ruble, please.

MANYUSHKA: No, they said you have to come yourself.

GAN-TSA-LIN: No can come, Manooska. You take.

MANYUSHKA: No, no, they want to see you mix it. They say it's too weak when you mix it here.

CHERUBIM: What? Morphine weak?

(Gan-Tsa-Lin says something in Chinese. Cherubim answers in Chinese.)

GAN-TSA-LIN: Manooska, he go. He can do.

MANYUSHKA: Are you sure he knows how?

GAN-TSA-LIN: Knows how. Don't worry. Turn round now—sure, sure.

MANYUSHKA: What are you hiding, Gasoline? I know all your secrets.

(Gan-Tsa-Lin turns Manyushka around.)

ACT I

GAN-TSA-LIN: So, Manooska, no peek! *(To Cherubim.)* You watch door! *(He gets a little box from a shelf in the corner, and a little vial, and wraps them up in a bundle of laundry. He speaks to Cherubim in Chinese.)*

CHERUBIM: Know how! No teach! We go, Manooska.

GAN-TSA-LIN: *(To Cherubim.)* You be good now! Bring back five rubles! Good-bye, Manooska! When you marry me?

MANYUSHKA: Huh? What makes you think I'd marry you?

GAN-TSA-LIN: Ah, Manooska! You know.

CHERUBIM: Nice girl, Manooska.

GAN-TSA-LIN: You shut up! Go! Go! Follow order! Keep eye on him, Manooska! *(To Cherubim.)* You take laundry!

CHERUBIM: Why you yell poor Chinaman? *(He picks up the laundry bundle.)*

MANYUSHKA: Yes, why scold him? He has the face of a little cherub.

GAN-TSA-LIN: Little cherub? He bandit!

MANYUSHKA: Good-bye, Gasoline.

GAN-TSA-LIN: Good-bye, Manooska. Come back soon. I have treat for you!

(Gan-Tsa-Lin attempts to kiss Manyushka good-bye.)

MANYUSHKA: Kiss a lady's hand, Gasoline, don't lunge at her lips! Let's go!

(Manyushka exits with Cherubim.)

GAN-TSA-LIN: Nice girl, Manooska! *(Sings softly to himself, a sad melody, in Chinese.)* Ummm, Manooska, could eat up!

(The lamp and the alcohol burner go out. Darkness. The Chinese laundry disappears.)

SCENE THREE
The Apartment.

(An alcohol burner comes up in Zoya's bedroom, followed by the lights in the rest of the apartment. Abolyaninov is on the bed, with Zoya leaning over him. Cherubim waits nearby, with a towel and a tray.)

ZOYA: Be patient, Pavlik, one moment.

(Zoya gives Abolyaninov a shot of morphine.)

ABOLYANINOV: *(After a pause.)* There. *(Reviving.)* There. *(He has revived.)* There. "They remind me...of another life...a distant shore." Why did you shut out the sunset, Zoyka? I didn't get to see it. Open the blinds, open them.

ZOYA: *(Opening them.)* Yes, of course.

(A May evening. The lights of the city begin to sparkle.)

ABOLYANINOV: Oh, look! How beautiful! What a wonderful street this is!... "...another life...a distant shore..." What a lovely voice that was...

(Cherubim turns off the burner. Abolyaninov rolls down his sleeve and fastens his cuff link. Zoya watches him.)

What do I owe you, my dear Chinaman?

CHERUBIM: Seven ruble.

ZOYA: Seven? Last time it was five. Thieves!

ABOLYANINOV: It's all right, Zoya, never mind. He's a fine Chinese fellow. *(He pats his pockets, looking for the money.)*

ZOYA. Wait, Pavlik. Allow me.

(She gives the money to Cherubim.)

CHERUBIM: Thank you...

ABOLYANINOV: Look, Zoya! What a smile! A real cherub! What a talented Chinaman!

CHERUBIM: Yes, talent—sure, sure... *(Intimately, to Abolyaninov.)* You like, I bring. Bring every day, you like. You no tell Gan-Tsa-Lin!...Bring everything. Morphine, alcohol...you like, I make picture for you. Very pretty. *(He bares his chest and reveals his tattoo, a ferocious dragon; and he himself becomes somehow strange and terrible.)*

ABOLYANINOV: That's amazing! Look, Zoyka!

ZOYA: How terrifying! Did you do that yourself?

CHERUBIM: Myself. In Shanghai.

ABOLYANINOV: Listen, my cherub, come every day, will you? I'm not a well man and I have to have my morphine. You can prepare it.

CHERUBIM: Sure, sure. Nice apartment. Poor Chinaman like.

ZOYA: Be careful, Pavlik. We don't know anything about him.

ABOLYANINOV: Oh, Zoyka, what are you saying! Just look at him! What a good, honest Chinese face! Listen, my angel, you don't belong to the Party, do you?

CHERUBIM: Sure, sure—wash clothes.

ZOYA: You wash clothes? Come back in an hour. Maybe you can do the ironing for my workshop.

CHERUBIM: I come...

ABOLYANINOV: You know, Zoyka...I want to give him a pair of trousers.

ZOYA: Don't be silly, Pavlik! He's fine the way he is.

ABOLYANINOV: Well, all right. Some other time. Come back now, don't forget. Good-bye, Chinaman. You will come back, won't you?

CHERUBIM: *(Smiling.)* Nice apartment.

ZOYA: *(Calling.)* Manyushka! Show him out.

MANYUSHKA: *(Appears.)* Let's go.

(She and Cherubim cross into the hallway.)

CHERUBIM: Good-bye, Manooska. Back one hour. I come everyday, Manooska. Work for Aboyanoo.

MANYUSHKA: Doing what?

ACT I

CHERUBIM: Bring medicine—sure, sure. Kiss, Manooska.

MANYUSHKA: Fat chance. On your way! *(She opens the door.)*

CHERUBIM: *(Mysteriously.)* When I rich, you kiss me. Aboyanoo give me trouser, I be so pretty…

MANYUSHKA: Whatever you say. Go, go…

(Cherubim leaves.)

He's one of a kind! *(She goes back to the kitchen.)*

ABOLYANINOV: "They remind me…"

ZOYA: Pavlik…I got the permit, Pavlik.

(Pause.)

Why don't you answer when a lady speaks to you, Count?

ABOLYANINOV: Forgive me, I was lost in thought. Did you say, "Count?" Please don't call me "Count" any more.

ZOYA: Why not?

ABOLYANINOV: I had a visitor today, a big lummox in tall boots, reeking of vodka. He came into my room and walked right up to me. "You're a former Count, aren't you?" he asked. "I beg your pardon," I said, "what does that mean exactly, 'a former Count?' Did I vanish into thin air? Here I stand, as a matter of fact, before your very eyes…"

ZOYA: And then what, Pavlik?

ABOLYANINOV: Can you imagine how he answered me? "You ought to be put in a Museum of the Revolution," he said, and he flipped his cigarette butt on my rug.

ZOYA: And then what?

ABOLYANINOV: On my way here, on the streetcar, as I passed the Zoological Gardens, I saw a sign: "Special attraction! Come in and see the former chicken!" I was intrigued. I got off and spoke to the guard. "Be so good as to tell me, please, what is she now, under the Soviet System?" "Who?" he asked. "The chicken," I said. "Well," he answered, "she's a rooster now." It seems that one of these thugs, a Communist professor, no less, has performed some sort of nasty experiment on the unhappy chicken as the result of which she has become a rooster...A red, red rooster...I swear to you, my head began to spin. I got on the next streetcar, rode along a little farther, and imagined that I saw...a former tiger. It's probably an elephant by now. What a nightmare!

ZOYA: You're one of a kind, Pavlik!

ABOLYANINOV: The former Pavlik.

ZOYA: Oh, my dear, sweet, darling, my former Pavlik, why don't you come live here with me?

ABOLYANINOV: No, my dearest Zoyka, thank you, but I can only live on Ostozhenka Street. My family has lived on Ostozhenka Street since 1625...for three hundred years.

ZOYA: I'll have to ask Lizanka, then, or Mymra, and I really don't want to.

(Pause.)

Well, Pavlik, it's time for you to make up your mind. Are you

ACT I

going to join me...*(In a whisper.)*...in the new business?
Remember, we're broke.

ABOLYANINOV: Yes, I'll join you. I agree... "They remind me..."

ZOYA: I had to bribe Aliluya today, so I only have 300 rubles left.
That'll get us started. The apartment, that's all we have. And I'll
squeeze everything I can out of it. We'll be in Paris by Christmas.

ABOLYANINOV: Yes, all right. I can't bear the sight of these former
chickens! I've got to get out of here, whatever it takes.

ZOYA: I know, I know. You're wasting away here. I'll save you, I'll take
you to Nice.

ABOLYANINOV: No, Zoya, I can't let you do that. But how I can be of
any use to you in this new business of yours, I can't imagine.

ZOYA: You'll play the piano.

ABOLYANINOV: But Zoya...they will offer me tips. I can't fight a duel
with everyone who tries to give me twenty kopecks.

ZOYA: Oh, Pavlik, you really do belong in a museum. You must take
whatever they give you. Every kopeck counts. We'll be in Paris
by Christmas. We'll have a million francs, I guarantee it.

*(In the distance we hear a voice like a caress, accompanied by a
piano, singing:*
    "Let us go, and leave this land,
    Land of pain and sorrow..."
The song breaks off abruptly.)

ABOLYANINOV: But how will we convert our rubles?

ZOYA: Goos will help us!

ABOLYANINOV: What about visas? They'll never give me a visa.

ZOYA: Goos!

ABOLYANINOV: Goos…Goos Almighty!…The former goose…He's probably an eagle by now.

ZOYA: *(Laughing.)* Oh, Pavlik…

ABOLYANINOV: I'm thirsty, Zoya. Do you have any beer?

ZOYA: *(Calling.)* Manyushka!

MANYUSHKA: *(Appearing.)* Yes, Zoya Denisovna?

ZOYA: Go out and get us some beer, please. And don't dawdle.

MANYUSHKA: Right away. *(She darts through the living room to the hallway, throws on a scarf, and runs out, forgetting to lock the door.)*

ABOLYANINOV: *(In a conspiratorial tone.)* And Manyushka? Is she in on it?

ZOYA: Of course. I have complete confidence in Manyushka. She'd go through fire and water for me.

ABOLYANINOV: Who else?

ZOYA: *(Also conspiratorial.)* Lizanka, Mymra, Madame Ivanova…

ABOLYANINOV: All of a sudden, I'm frightened, Zoyka. What if we get caught?

ACT I

ZOYA: If we're smart, we won't get caught. We'd better talk in there, Pavlik, in the mythical being's room. Not out here. Not with the windows open.

(Zoya and Abolyaninov cross the living room and go into the mythical being's room, closing the door behind them. We can still hear their voices faintly through the door. We can also hear someone coming up the stairs and singing, in a thin voice, with ridiculous emotion:
"High above the stars were shining,
As the frost began to scold,
When up walked...")

AMETISTOV: *(Stepping into the hallway.)*
"...a tiny baby,
(Sadly.)
Turning blue, so lost and cold!"
(He sets his battered suitcase on the floor and looks around. He's wearing torn trousers; a filthy military-style jacket with four pockets, with a medal pinned on the chest; and a cap.) Whew! Son-of-a-bitch! Dragging myself all the way from Kursk Station, up five long flights, lugging this old suitcase of mine! That's no small feat, believe you me...two whole miles, at least!...What I'd give for a bottle of beer!...Oh, my Destiny, how cruel to bring me here again. So what are your plans for me now? *(He looks into the kitchen.)* Comrades! Hello! Anybody home? Zoya Denisovna, are you here? Hmm...*(He looks into the living room, crosses to the mythical being's room, and hears the voices.)*...Oh-ho-ho! *(He opens the door a crack and eavesdrops.)*

ABOLYANINOV: *(Off.)* No, Zoya, not me, I'd be hopeless. The position requires an accomplished rascal.

AMETISTOV: *(To himself.)* Just in time!

(Manyushka comes back with beer.)

MANYUSHKA: Oh, dear! Did I forget to close the door?

(Ametistov eases shut the door to the mythical being's room and returns to the hallway.)

Who are you? What do you want?

AMETISTOV: *Pardon, pardon!* Don't be frightened, comrade. That's not really beer, is it? What a miracle! I've been dreaming about beer all the way from Kursk Station!

MANYUSHKA: Are you looking for somebody?

AMETISTOV: For Zoya Denisovna, of course. And with whom do I have the pleasure of speaking?

MANYUSHKA: I am Zoya Denisovna's niece.

AMETISTOV: Well, well, well...how delightful!...I had no idea Zoyechka had such a lovely niece. I am Zoya Denisovna's cousin.

(Ametistov kisses Manyushka's hand.)

MANYUSHKA: *(Dumfounded.)* Zoya Denisovna! Zoya Denisovna!

(She runs into the living room. Ametistov runs after her with his suitcase. Zoya and Abolyaninov enter.)

AMETISTOV: My dear little cousin, *je vous salue!*

(Zoya stands amazed.)

Well, introduce us, cousin dear...

ZOYA: You?...Is it really you?...Yes, of course...Pavel Fyodorovich, this is my cousin Ametistov.

24

ACT I

AMETISTOV: *Pardon, pardon. (To Abolyaninov.)* I am Putinkovsky! Non-Party. A former nobleman.

ABOLYANINOV: *(Astonished.)* A pleasure.

AMETISTOV: Cousin dear, may I have two words with you, *à part,* as they say?

ZOYA: Excuse me, Pavlik. I must have two words with Aleksander Tarasovich.

AMETISTOV: *Pardon, pardon.* I'm Vassily Ivanovich…We've been separated for such a brief time, cousin dear, and you don't even remember my name! Oh, that breaks my heart. Shame on you!…

ABOLYANINOV: I'll be in the other room…*(He disappears.)*

ZOYA: Manyushka, take a beer to Pavel Fyodorovich.

(Manyushka exits. Pause.)

I thought they shot you in Baku…

AMETISTOV: *Pardon, pardon.* So what? So they shot me in Baku. Does that mean I can't come back to Moscow? It was all a big mistake anyway, they didn't mean it…

ZOYA: My head is spinning…

AMETISTOV: With joy?

ZOYA: I don't understand a thing…

AMETISTOV: Well, I was spared—in the May Day amnesty, of course…By the way, when did you acquire a niece?

ZOYA: A niece? Oh, you mean Manyushka. She's my maid.

AMETISTOV: Say no more, cousin. To protect your space allocation. *(Shouting.)* Manyushka!

(Manyushka appears, flustered.)

How about a beer for me, too? I'm dying for one! And just what kind of a niece are you anyway, you little devil?

(Manyushka exits, stricken.)

Can you believe it, I even kissed her hand? What a scandal!

ZOYA: Where are you staying? There's a housing crisis in Moscow, you know.

AMETISTOV: I know. That's why I'm staying here.

ZOYA: Oh, no, you're not.

AMETISTOV: Oh, Zoyka, how rude! Well, if that's the way you feel, go ahead, be rude. Turn away your poor cousin who dragged himself up here all the way from Kursk Station. An orphan, too! Fine, what difference does it make? I'm nobody. I'll go...But you'll be sorry, cousin dear...

ZOYA: Are you trying to scare me? It won't work!

AMETISTOV: Why should I try to scare you? I'm a decent fellow, *un gentilhomme,* as they say!....*(Whispering.)*...but I wouldn't be Ametistov, would I, if I didn't go straight to the GPU and file an official report on just what kind of workshop you're really planning to set up in your cozy apartment...Oh, yes, my dear Zoya Denisovna, I heard everything. *(He starts to leave.)*

ACT I

ZOYA: Wait. How did you get in, anyway? I didn't hear the doorbell.

AMETISTOV: *La porte était ouverte!*...But I haven't even smothered you with kisses yet, my darling cousin...

ZOYA: *(Pushing him away.)* It's my fate—I'm stuck with you!

(Manyushka enters with a bottle of beer and a glass.)

Manyushka, did you forget to lock the door? Oh, Manyushka! ...Well, never mind, go and apologize to Pavel Fyodorovich.

(Manyushka leaves. Ametistov drinks his beer.)

AMETISTOV: Aaaah, Moscow! Such wonderful beer! So, you managed to hold on to the apartment, Zoyka. Good for you!

ZOYA: It's my fate! I can't escape it...

AMETISTOV: What are you trying to do? Hurt my feelings and make me go away?

ZOYA: Just tell me what you want.

AMETISTOV: First, a pair of pants!

ZOYA: Are those all you have? What's in your suitcase?

AMETISTOV: In my suitcase? Six decks of cards, and postcard portraits of our beloved leaders, bless their hearts! They kept me from starving. I came on a mail train, all the way to Moscow from Baku—and that's no picnic, I can tell you....Anyway, I borrowed the postcards, you know what I mean, from the Baku Cultural Center, as mementos, and I let them go for twenty kopecks each.

27

ZOYA: You're really something!

AMETISTOV: So good, this beer... "Comrade, buy a postcard!"...One poor guy bought five. "I'll give them to my relatives," he said. "They love our leaders."

ZOYA: And the decks of cards? All marked, of course.

AMETISTOV: What do you take me for, *madame?*

ZOYA: I know you, Ametistov! So...what have you been up to these past seven years?

AMETISTOV: Oh, cousin!...In 1919, I'm Director-in-Chief of the Chernigov Bureau of Art and Culture...

(Zoya laughs.)

But here come the Whites...So the Reds give me money to evacuate to Moscow, but I head for Rostov, instead, and go to work for the Whites...Pretty soon, here come the Reds again!...So the Whites give me money to evacuate, but I go back to the Reds, and become the Chief of their Political Agitation Corps. But here come the Whites again! The Reds cover my Evacuation Expenses, of course, but this time I head for the Whites in the Crimea. So now I'm the manager of a little restaurant in Sevastopol, where I get involved in a friendly game of *chemin de fer* and drop 300,000 rubles in a single night...

ZOYA: Oh? They must have been experts.

AMETISTOV: Savages, I'm telling you, degenerates, a real bunch of thieves!...Oh, well, you know the rest...more Whites, more Reds, and there I go, bouncing around the whole Soviet System. In Stavropol, I'm an actor. In Novocherkask, a musician—in the Fire Department Band. In Voronezh, they put me in charge of the Food Supply…my career was no longer advancing, I had to admit it…so I decided it was about time to reach out for the Party line…To tell you the truth, I almost sank without a ripple. My problem was how to cut through all the red tape and acquire the necessary credentials…but how, how…? When suddenly, out of the blue, a friend of mine named Chemodanov perished in my room…What a splendid fellow he was, Karl Petrovich… and a party member, too…

ZOYA: In Voronezh?

AMETISTOV: No, I'm in Odessa now. Why should the Party be the loser, I thought. One man falls, another takes his place, like legionnaires. So I shed a few tears over the fallen hero, appropriate his Party card, and set off for Baku. Here's a sleepy little oil town, I thought, I can start up a *chemin de fer* game and set this place on fire. So I go around passing myself off as Chemodanov. But the next thing you know—bang!—my door flies open, it's an old pal of Chemodanov's! What a scene!! He's got nine and I've got nothing! Busted! I head for the window…but we're three floors up.

ZOYA: What a story!

AMETISTOV: A little bad luck, Zoyechka, what can you do? I didn't draw the card I needed…but I made such an eloquent summation at the trial that even my guards were sobbing!…So they shot me…Well, that finished me in the provinces. What next? When every other road is a dead end, you have to head for Moscow. And now that I'm here, where's the Zoyka I used to know? You've grown callous, way up here in your big apartment!…You've cut yourself off from the masses!

ZOYA: All right, that's enough. What did you hear?

AMETISTOV: I was just lucky, Zoyechka!

ZOYA: You can stay.

AMETISTOV: Zoyechka!

ZOYA: Shut up! You can be the manager of my new business.

AMETISTOV: Oh, Zoyechka!

ZOYA: But I don't even want to hear the word "cards" in this apartment. Is that clear?

AMETISTOV: What is she trying to do to me, comrades? Oh, Zoya, that's not the correct Marxist interpretation. This apartment was made for cards.

ZOYA: No cards.

AMETISTOV: Awwww...

ZOYA: Watch out, Ametistov. If you pull any of your old tricks, I'll get you. You've told me too much.

AMETISTOV: Apparently, I have confided my melancholy saga to a snake! *Mon Dieu!*

ZOYA: Shut up! You're such a fool! And where, by the way, is my necklace? The one you promised to sell for me just before you left town?

AMETISTOV: Your necklace? Wait, wait...Oh, you mean the one with the little diamonds?

ZOYA: You son-of-a-bitch!

AMETISTOV: *Merci, merci.* So this is how Zoyechka welcomes her relatives!

ZOYA: Do you have any papers?

AMETISTOV: I have a pocketful of papers. It's only a question of which is the freshest, so to speak...*(He pulls out some papers.)* Karl Chemodanov—not worth talking about! Siguradze, Anton... no, that's no good.

ZOYA: This is like a bad dream. You said you were Putinkovsky!

AMETISTOV: No, Zoyechka, I got mixed up. That's out. The real Putinkovsky lives in Moscow. Maybe I should go back to my own name, for a change. Surely after eight years, Moscow has forgotten me. Why not? Put me down as Ametistov. Wait a second, they'll ask you about my military service...I have a Hernia Exemption, somewhere...*(He takes out a paper.)*

ZOYA: *(Taking a splendid pair of trousers out of the wardrobe.)* Here, put these on.

AMETISTOV: God will bless you for this, Zoyechka. No peeking!

ZOYA: I'll try to restrain myself. The trousers belong to Pavel Fyodorovich. Make sure you return them.

AMETISTOV: Your morganatic consort?

ZOYA: Don't be cute. He's my...husband!

AMETISTOV: What's his name?

ZOYA: Abolyaninov.

AMETISTOV: A Count! Well, well, what a catch!... *(He quickly takes off his medal and slips it in his pocket.)* Congratulations, cousin! Although he probably hasn't got a kopeck left. A counter-revolutionary, by the look of him... *(He admires his new trousers in the mirror.)* What noble trousers! In trousers like these, you feel as if you're strutting back and forth on the station platform, with everyone staring at you.

ZOYA: And get your aliases straightened out. You're putting me in a ridiculous position...

(Abolyaninov comes in.)

Ah, Pavlik! Forgive us for taking so long, my dear. We were talking business.

AMETISTOV: We got lost in the memories of our childhood...We grew up together, you know, didn't we, Zoyechka? A moment ago, I was actually weeping...You're looking at the trousers?... *Pardon, pardon,* I was robbed on my way to Moscow...My other suitcase disappeared in Taganrog...Oh, how embarrassing!...I'm sure you don't mind. Among members of the nobility, it's a trifle...

ABOLYANINOV: Please, please, of course...

ZOYA: Pavlik, Aleksander Tarasovich is going to be our new manager, if that meets with your approval.

ABOLYANINOV: By all means...if you recommend...Vassily Ivanovich for...

AMETISTOV: *Pardon, pardon,* that's my stage name. I'm Aleksander Tarasovich...Does that surprise you? On stage, Vassily Ivanovich Putinkovsky! Off stage, Aleksander Tarasovich Ametistov. A name all-too-famous now, alas, since so many of us have been dragged in front of Bolshevik firing squads...What a novel this would make! You'll be sobbing when I tell you...

ABOLYANINOV: I look forward to it. Where do you come from?

AMETISTOV: Me? Where do I come from? From Baku, most recently, where they were treating me for my rheumatism. But that's another novel. You'll be sobbing when I tell you…

ABOLYANINOV: Are you non-Party, may I ask?

AMETISTOV: *Quelle question!* How can you even ask?

ABOLYANINOV: I thought I saw…on your chest…some kind of a…but I must have imagined it.

AMETISTOV: Yes, of course, but that's only for traveling. It works like a charm…train tickets without waiting in line, all kinds of things…

MANYUSHKA: *(Appearing.)* Aliluya is here.

ZOYA: Send him in. *(To Ametistov.)* He's the Chairman of the Apartment House Committee, so watch your step.

ALILUYA: *(Entering.)* Good evening. Hello, Citizen Abolyaninov. Well, Zoya Denisovna, how about it? Have you decided on a new tenant?

ZOYA: Yes. Here are the papers. Register my cousin, Aleksander Tarasovich Ametistov. He's just arrived. He's going to manage the workshop.

ALILUYA: Oh, is that so?

AMETISTOV: Yes, of course…I'm an old hand at needlework. And may I offer you a glass of beer, my esteemed comrade?

ALILUYA: *Merci.* Don't mind if I do. It was so hot today, and with all my responsibilities, I never got a chance to sit down.

AMETISTOV: Well, you know what they say about the weather…and you have such a huge building here, dear comrade…really enormous!

ALILUYA: Don't remind me—it's sheer torture. Have you got a Hernia Exemption?

AMETISTOV: Yes, I do. *(He hands him the paper.)* And you, comrade, you belong to the Party, don't you?

ALILUYA: I'm a sympathizer.

AMETISTOV: Well. That's good. *(He puts on his medal again.)* I'm a former Party member myself. *(Aside to Abolyaninov.) Devant les gens…*a useful subterfuge…

ALILUYA: Why a "former" Party member?

AMETISTOV: I couldn't stand all that petty wrangling of a factional nature. Oh, there's a lot I can't agree with…I looked around and saw that things weren't working out as planned! So I stood up and told them, right to their faces…

ALILUYA: Did you really?

AMETISTOV: Why not? After all, I'm an old warrior. I had nothing to lose but my chains!…Ah, once upon a time, I played a pivotal part in the Caucasus. "No," I told them, "this is not right! In the first place, you're all deviating! And in the second place, you are violating the purity of the Party line. You are betraying our theory!" "So that's how you feel!" they said. "Then take that!…and this!…and that!" What hot-tempered people they can be…Your health!

ABOLYANINOV: *(To Zoya.)* He's a genius, no doubt about it!

ZOYA: *(Softly.)* An absolute scoundrel!…That's enough politics now! Well, Comrade Aliluya, tomorrow's the big day. I'm opening my workshop.

AMETISTOV: And we're off! To the success of the workshop and the health of our leader, Zoya Denisovna—Comrade Peltz! Oo-rah! *(He drinks some beer.)* And now, to the health of our esteemed Apartment House Committee Chairman and party sympathizer…*(Softly.)*…What's his name?

ZOYA: *(Softly.)* Anisim Zotikovich Aliluya.

AMETISTOV: That's what I'm saying! Aliluya! Aliluya! A-li-lu-ya! Oo-rah!

(From the courtyard a group of boys begins to sing the familiar song of ceremonial tribute:
    "Long life to you, and
    Long life to you, and…")

My sentiments exactly! Long life, long life, long life!

CURTAIN

ACT II

Scene One
The Apartment.

(The living room has been transformed into a needlecraft workshop, with a portrait of Karl Marx hanging on the wall. Mannequins with blank doll faces preside over the billowing fabrics. The Seamstress works away at her sewing machine. The Cutter stands with a tape measure draped around her neck, assisting the First and Second Ladies, as the Third Lady waits her turn.)

FIRST LADY: Oh, no, my dear, this won't do at all. I look like I'm missing two ribs. Let it out, for heaven's sake, let it out!

THE CUTTER: Certainly.

SECOND LADY: *(Chattering to the Third Lady.)* You'll never believe it!—She says, "I can't do a thing with you, *madame,* until you have your hair bobbed." So I ran right over to Jean—you know the one I mean, on Arbat Street—begged him to take me, ran right back, and she slapped on a bonnet—well, you should have seen me—I looked like I had my head in a kettle.

(The Third Lady giggles.)

You think that's funny, my dear? As a matter of fact, it's very sad.

FIRST LADY: Surely it's not supposed to stick out like that?

THE CUTTER: Where, *madame!*

SECOND LADY: What nerve she has! "It's because your cheekbones are a little too large," she says.

(The doorbell rings.)

AMETISTOV: *(Dashing through.) Pardon, pardon,* I'm not looking…

SECOND LADY: *Monsieur* Ametistov…

AMETISTOV: *Votre serviteur, madame.*

SECOND LADY: What's your opinion? Are my cheekbones too large?

AMETISTOV: *Qu'est-ce que vous dites, madame?* You have no cheek-bones at all. *Pardon, pardon. (He dashes off.)*

FIRST LADY: Who *is* that?

THE CUTTER: He's the manager of our needlecraft school and work-shop.

FIRST LADY: It's an impressive establishment.

AMETISTOV: *(At the front door.)* Sorry, comrade, there's not a thing I can do for you. *"Absolument!"* If you had a certificate from the Commissariat of Labor, of course, I could put you right to work.

FIRST FEMALE VOICE: When I ask them for a certificate, they say, "But you don't have a job!" When I ask you for a job, you say, "But you don't have a certificate!" What do you recommend I do next, hang myself?

AMETISTOV: *"Pardon, pardon."* What a thing to say! It's the law, you know, and to me the law is sacred. Bye-bye. *(He returns to the living room, on the run.) "Pardon, pardon,"* I'm not looking…Oh, that manteau is magnificent!

FIRST LADY: What's magnificent about it? *(She looks into the mirror.)* Does my bottom really stick out like that?

AMETISTOV: You have an absolutely perfect bottom.

THE SEAMSTRESS: *(Aside, to The Cutter.)* She has a bottom like a grand piano. Sew on a few keys and we'll give a recital.

THE CUTTER: *(Quietly.)* Shhhh, Varvara Nikanorovna. *(To the First Lady.)* I'll let it out a little at the side.

(The doorbell rings.)

AMETISTOV: *(Under his breath.)* Oh, shut up. *(To the Ladies.) Pardon, pardon!* I can't see a thing! *(He flies away.)*

THIRD LADY: He's as busy as a bee.

AMETISTOV: *(At the front door.)* So, you're looking for a job? Are you a member of the union?

SECOND FEMALE VOICE: *(Off.)* I am.

AMETISTOV: *(At the door.)* May I ask, dear comrade, if you have a certificate from the Commissariat of Labor?

SECOND FEMALE VOICE: *(Off, triumphantly.)* I do! Yes, yes, I do!

AMETISTOV: *(At the door.)* Ah...what a shame! We don't have any openings.

SECOND FEMALE VOICE: *(Off; stunned.)* You don't? But I have a recommendation from the Party!

AMETISTOV: But of course! We don't take anybody without a recommendation from the Party. *"C'est impossible!"*

SECOND LADY: Shouldn't this go all the way around?

THE CUTTER: That would make you look even bigger.

SECOND LADY: Then don't do it!

THIRD LADY: Plump people should stay away from wraparounds.

SECOND LADY: Oh? You should know…

SECOND FEMALE VOICE: *(Off.)* Well, that's it then, I guess. Good-bye.

AMETISTOV: *(At the door.)* Bye-bye, dear comrade. *(Flying through.)* *Pardon, pardon!* I'm not looking.

THIRD LADY: What a thriving business! *Madame* Peltz is doing very well.

THE CUTTER: *(Helping the First Lady off with her manteau.)* All right then, we'll let it out for you.

FIRST LADY: And please, my dear, make sure it's ready by Wednesday.

THE CUTTER: Wednesday is not possible, *madame.* Varvara Nikanorovna will never have it ready by then.

FIRST LADY: Oh, my God, that's terrible! *(To The Seamstress.)* Varvara Nikanorovna! Please, my little dove, by Wednesday!

THE SEAMSTRESS: Impossible, *madame.* There are six ahead of you. *(She continues sewing.)*

FIRST LADY: Oh, that's awful!…What about Friday?

THE SEAMSTRESS: I'll do my best. *(She continues sewing.)*

FIRST LADY: Well, that's all I can ask. Good-bye, *Monsieur* Ametistov.

AMETISTOV: *Au revoir, madame, enchanté!*

(The First Lady goes out.)

SECOND LADY: Please tell me, *Monsieur* Ametistov, what looks better on me? The loose wraparound or the tight wraparound?

AMETISTOV: You look terrific however you're wrapped.

(The doorbell rings. Ametistov and Manyushka, who enters, both cross toward the door.)

Don't let anyone else in, Comrade Manyushka, it's eight o'clock already. *(From the hall.)* Oh, how nice to see you!

MANYUSHKA: Zoya Denisovna! Agnessa Ferapontovna is here! *(She goes off.)*

AMETISTOV: Welcome, Agnessa Ferapontovna! Come in, come in!

AGNESSA FERAPONTOVNA: *(Coming in with a parcel.)* Hello, Comrade Ametistov.

AMETISTOV: Please, sit down, make yourself at home.

AGNESSA FERAPONTOVNA: Thank you, but I can only stay a minute. *(To The Cutter.)* Hello, my dear.

THE CUTTER: Good evening, Agnessa Ferapontovna.

ZOYA: *(Entering.)* Oh, what a wonderful surprise!

AGNESSA FERAPONTOVNA: Hello, Zoya dear.

ZOYA: *(Quietly, to the Third Lady.)* Please let us take Agnessa Ferapontovna next. She doesn't have much time.

THIRD LADY: Why should I?

AMETISTOV: *(Whispering to her.)* Well...she's the wife of...

SECOND LADY: *(Overhearing him.)* She can go ahead of me—I'm not in a hurry.

THIRD LADY: Never mind, my dear, she's going ahead of me.

ZOYA: Please, Agnessa Ferapontovna...

AGNESSA FERAPONTOVNA: Thank you so much. I have a car waiting. *(Opening her parcel and taking out a dress.)* Look here...this bow is way too low, don't you think? It spoils the whole effect.

SECOND LADY: Oh, what a beautiful gown! Is it from Paris?

AGNESSA FERAPONTOVNA: Paris, yes.

THE CUTTER: That's easy to fix...can you slip it on for me?

AGNESSA FERAPONTOVNA: No, no, I don't have time.

THE CUTTER: That's all right, we'll use a mannequin.

AMETISTOV: *Un moment, madame. (He slips the dress on a mannequin.)*

SECOND LADY: Excuse me, *madame,* when were you in Paris?

AGNESSA FERAPONTOVNA: Two weeks ago. *(To The Seamstress.)* There, my dear. That's where it should go.

SECOND LADY: Forgive me, but could I ask a little favor of you? You see, I'm also planning a trip to Paris and, uh...I wonder if your husband could help with our visas? My husband—sorry, my name is Sepoorakhina—he's not actually in the Party, but he does have a very important job with the State Electric Bureau.

AGNESSA FERAPONTOVNA: Pardon me, but I'm in a terrible hurry. Unfortunately, my husband can't help you. He has nothing to do with visas. *(To Zoya.)* I have a big favor to ask of you, Zoya Denisovna. Can you have this ready by tomorrow?

ZOYA: Of course we can. Varvara Nikanorovna?

THE SEAMSTRESS: Of course we can.

AGNESSA FERAPONTOVNA: Thank you so much. Good-bye, Zoya Denisovna.

SECOND LADY: Pardon me for being so forward, but which way are you going?

AGNESSA FERAPONTOVNA: *(Surprised.)* To the Kuznetsky Bridge.

SECOND LADY: Me, too! May I walk with you?

AMETISTOV: *(Aside.)* What a bitch! Like a leech!

AGNESSA FERAPONTOVNA: Thank you, but I have a car. *(She goes out.)*

AMETISTOV: Agnessa Ferapontovna has a car.

SECOND LADY: I'll just see her down the stairs then. *(She hurries out.)*

THIRD LADY: Terrible, just terrible…

THE SEAMSTRESS: The grip of a bulldog. *(She giggles.)*

THIRD LADY: Well, I'll go, too. I'll come back tomorrow. How much do I owe you, Zoya Denisovna?

ZOYA: Eighty-five rubles.

THIRD LADY: Here's fifty. I'll bring the rest on Tuesday. Is that all right?

ZOYA: Of course.

THIRD LADY: Good-bye, Zoya Denisovna. *(She rushes out.)*

ZOYA: Is there anybody else?

THE CUTTER: No, she's the last.

ZOYA: Good. *(She leaves.)*

AMETISTOV: Whew! We made it! Closing time!

(The Seamstress and The Cutter get ready to leave.)

THE SEAMSTRESS: We must have had thirty people today.

AMETISTOV: "Rest well!" dear comrades, as the Work Code specifies. "make good use of your leisure time!" It's a golden autumn, go out to the Sparrow Hills…

THE SEAMSTRESS: Hills, Aleksander Tarasovich! I'll be lucky if I can climb into my bed!

AMETISTOV: Oh, I know just what you mean! All I can think about is lying down. I'll crawl into bed, curl up with my History of Materialistic Philosophy, and go right to sleep! Don't bother straightening up, Varvara Nikanorovna! Comrade Manyusha will take care of it.

THE CUTTER: Good-bye, Aleksander Tarasovich.

THE SEAMSTRESS: Good-bye.

(The Seamstress and The Cutter leave.)

AMETISTOV: All these damned women have worn me to a frazzle! Wherever I look, rumps and ribbons, ribbons and rumps! *(He takes out a bottle of cognac and pours himself a drink.)* Whew, what a bunch! Zoyechka! Dear lady-director!

ZOYA: *(Entering.)* What?

AMETISTOV: Here's what, cousin—and it's very important. We need Alla Vadimovna, and we need her now.

ZOYA: Don't count on her.

AMETISTOV: *Pardon, pardon…*Doesn't she owe you money?

ZOYA: Two thousand rubles.

AMETISTOV: Well, then, we've got her!

ZOYA: She'll pay it off.

AMETISTOV: She won't, I'm telling you. I can see it in her eyes. The eyes are the windows of the bank account. If you don't have any money, your eyes always give you away. I speak from personal experience. Whenever I'm broke, I'm melancholy, depressed, even drawn toward socialism. And when a woman gets that look in her eyes, believe me, she wants to escape from a union—either marital or Soviet. Alla Vadimovna is ready to listen…And what a magnificent creature she is! What an asset she'll be for the apartment! She and Madame Ivanova are a matched set. As for Lizanka and Mymra, all they can do is squeal. I can't run a first-class business, *chère maman,* with second-class people.

ACT II

(The doorbell rings.)

Who the hell can that be?…You better listen to Ametistov, he knows what he's doing. Ametistov thinks big.

MANYUSHKA: *(Entering.)* Alla Vadimovna is asking to see you.

AMETISTOV: *Voilà!* Squeeze her, now. Don't let her get away!

ZOYA: Calm down. *(To Manyushka.)* Send her in.

(Alla, a dazzlingly beautiful woman, enters.)

ALLA: Hello, Zoya Denisovna! Forgive me if I've come at a bad time.

ZOYA: No, no…I'm glad to see you. Come in.

AMETISTOV: May I kiss your hand, my adored Alla Vadimovna? *(He does so.)* And what can I say about your dress, except that it's enchanting!

ALLA: That's a compliment for Zoya Denisovna.

AMETISTOV: But when you see the gowns we just got in from *Paris,* you'll take yours off and toss it out the window. On the word of a former hussar!

ALLA: You were a hussar?

AMETISTOV: *Mais oui.* And now I must fly.

ALLA: You're always darting about, like a bee.

AMETISTOV: Well, you know what they say: "Shine over here, shine over there—spread your blessings everywhere!" *(To Zoya, quietly.)* Squeeze her, squeeze her…*(He winks at Zoya and disappears.)*

ALLA: What a remarkable manager, Zoya Denisovna. Is he really a former hussar?

ZOYA: Unfortunately, I cannot confirm that...Please sit down, Alla Vadimovna. Would you like some tea?

ALLA: No, thank you.

(Pause.)

ALLA: I have come on a very serious matter, Zoya Denisovna.

ZOYA: Yes?

ALLA: This is so difficult...I know I'm supposed to pay you today, but I wonder if I could have a little more time...

(Pause.)

...I've had some setbacks lately...I...I've never been...uh... this is so embarrassing...

(Pause.)

...Your silence is killing me, Zoya Denisovna.

ZOYA: What do you want me to say? This is very sad.

ALLA: Forgive me. I don't blame you for not answering. But I must ask you to wait two or three days, while I do everything in my power to get the money...I can't tell you how embarrassed I am.

(Pause.)

Good-bye, Zoya Denisovna.

ACT II

ZOYA: Good-bye.

(Alla crosses toward the door.)

Wait a minute, Alla Vadimovna. I thought you wanted to see the new gowns.

ALLA: What a cruel joke, Zoya Denisovna. I can't even pay for what I've already ordered, I don't know which way to turn, and you offer me...

ZOYA: Oh, Alla Vadimovna, what difference does it make? I'm not in much better shape myself. So what should I do, spend all my time crying. There are more important things than money, after all. I'll have to offer these gowns to undiscriminating vulgarians, and you're one of the few women in Moscow with real taste. It would be such a pleasure to show them to you. Take a look... *(She opens the wardrobe to reveal a dazzling array of Paris gowns.)*...Aren't they glorious? Evening gowns...

ALLA: Breathtaking! Are they Paquin's?...

ZOYA: They're Paquin's.

ALLA: I knew it as soon as I saw them. What an artist!

ZOYA: Not every woman has the figure for them...but they'd all be perfect on you. Here's the lilac gown...look how elegant the little belt is. So simple.

ALLA: Simplicity itself. How much is it?

ZOYA: Three hundred and twenty rubles.

(Pause.)

You poor baby, so you've gotten yourself in some kind of mess…

ALLA: Zoya Denisovna, I may owe you money, but that hardly gives you the right to take such a familiar tone with me.

ZOYA: Oh, come on, Allachka, don't be like that! I'm nice to you and you answer coldly. That's not right! If you had just come to me in a friendly way and said, "Things are tough right now, Zoya"…well, we could have worked something out…but instead you march in here like the Statue of Liberty—"*I'm* a great lady, and *you*, Zoya, you're nothing but a seamstress." If that's how you really feel, what can you expect from the seamstress?

ALLA: I swear to you, Zoya Denisovna, that's not how I feel at all. I'm just so embarrassed about my debt that I can hardly look at you.

ZOYA: All right, all right. Stop talking about your debt! So you have no money…Sit down. Tell me honestly, friend to friend: how much do you need?

ALLA: Too much. It's killing me.

ZOYA: Why do you need so much?

(*Pause.*)

ALLA: I want to go abroad.

ZOYA: I see. There's nothing to hold you here?

ALLA: Nothing.

ZOYA: But there must be…someone. You don't need to tell me who, but…can't he provide for you?

ALLA: Since the death of my husband, there has been no one, Zoya Denisovna.

ACT II

ZOYA: Oh, Alla!

ALLA: It's true.

ZOYA: It's hard to believe. How do you survive?

ALLA: By selling off my diamonds. But they're all gone now.

ZOYA: All right…we'll just have to find a way to get you some money.

ALLA: Zoya Denisovna!

ZOYA: Relax, my dear. Didn't you tell me, a few months ago, you were hoping to go to Paris. You applied for a visa. What happened?

ALLA: It was denied.

ZOYA: Well…I could get you one.

ALLA: If you could, I'd be grateful for the rest of my life.

ZOYA: I could even help you earn some money…enough to pay off all your debts.

ALLA: Oh, Zoyechka! How could I ever earn that kind of money in Moscow?

ZOYA: Why not? You can work here. You can be a model.

ALLA: A model? But, Zoyechka, models don't make that kind of money.

ZOYA: No? that depends…I'll give you a salary of a thousand rubles a month, cancel your debt, and help you get out of the country…Well?

(Pause.)

You'll work nights only, every other day...

(Pause.)

Well?

ALLA: *(Pulling away.)* Every other day? Nights only? How can that be?

ZOYA: In four months, it will be Christmas. In four months, you'll be free, you'll be out of debt, with plenty of money, and no one will ever know that Alla worked as a model. In the spring you will see the boulevards of Paris. And in springtime, the sky over Paris is lilac, Alla, lilac.

> *(We hear a voice singing softly, accompanied by piano*
> *"Let us go, and leave this land,*
> *Land of pain and sorrow...".)*

And the man you love...he's waiting for you there?

ALLA: Yes...

ZOYA: In the spring you'll be with him, beside him, on his arm, strolling down the *Champs Elysées,* and he will never, never know...

ALLA: *(Astonished.)* So that's what you call a workshop! Nights only...You know what you are, Zoyka?...You're the very devil!...And no one, no one, will ever know?

ZOYA: I swear it!

(Pause.)

ALLA: I'll start in three days.

ZOYA: *(Turning back to the wardrobe.)* Then take one, Allachka... whichever you like!

ALLA: The lilac. I'll take the lilac.

(Blackout. Zoya and Alla disappear.)

SCENE TWO
The apartment.

(The same day. Evening. A lamp in the living room comes up. Ametistov and Zoya are sitting beside it, Ametistov roaring with laughter.)

AMETISTOV: What did I tell you? A little credit, please, for Aleksander Ametistov!

ZOYA: Well, you're no fool.

AMETISTOV: Did you hear that, comrades? I'm no fool! I was right, wasn't I, Zoyechka? I know what I'm doing!

ZOYA: Yes, I have to admit it. You've improved with age—you're smarter.

AMETISTOV: And remember now, Zoyechka, you're going to owe at least half your fortune to this busy little brain of mine. You won't desert me, will you? You'll take me with you, won't you? Ah, Nice, Monte Carlo, when will I see you again? The azure sea, and strolling along beside it, me, in white trousers! No fool? I'm a genius!

ZOYA: Listen, genius, do me a favor: stop speaking French around Alla. You're driving her crazy.

AMETISTOV: What are you insinuating—that my French is bad?

ZOYA: It's not only bad, it's atrocious!

AMETISTOV: Oh, come on, Zoya! *Parole d'honneur!* I've been playing *chemin de fer* since I was ten years old, and you say my French is bad?

ZOYA: And one more thing. Why do you tell so many lies? Just what kind of hussar are you supposed to be, anyway?

AMETISTOV: And why do you get so much pleasure out of being mean? What a terrible disposition! If it was up to me, I'd send you to Siberia for your personality alone.

ZOYA: Since it's not up to you, you'd better get dressed. Goos will be here any minute. I'm going to change. *(She goes out.)*

AMETISTOV: Goos? Why didn't you say so! *(He begins to panic.)* Goos! Goos, everybody! Goos is coming! *(He fetches a stepladder and takes down the portrait of Karl Marx.)* Come on down, old man. Nothing more for you to see. Nothing you'd be interested in, I guarantee it. Now, where's my little Mister Bird's-Nest-Soup! *(Calling.)* Niece Manyushka!

MANYUSHKA: *(Appearing.)* What is it?

AMETISTOV: What exactly is going on back there, anyway? Just curious. Am I supposed to do everything myself?

MANYUSHKA: I'm washing the dishes!

AMETISTOV: The dishes can wait. Help me!

(Ametistov and Manyushka miraculously transform the apartment into an atelier. Abolyaninov enters, in a full dress suit.)

ABOLYANINOV: *(To Ametistov.)* Good evening.

AMETISTOV: Greetings, maestro.

ABOLYANINOV: Excuse me, I've been meaning to ask you for some time, please address me by my name and patronymic.

AMETISTOV: Now why in the world should that bother you, you silly thing? The men in our circle always…uh…what do you have against "maestro," anyway?

ABOLYANINOV: It's such a peculiar appellation. It grates on me, like "comrade."

AMETISTOV: *Pardon, pardon.* "Maestro," "comrade"—there's a big difference…Bring out the nymph, Manyushka.

MANYUSHKA: Here she is. *(From behind a curtain she takes out a painting of a nude woman. She giggles.)*

AMETISTOV: Now, that's more like it! What a charming picture! Well, Count, how about that? Make you jealous, Manyushka?

MANYUSHKA: Shame on you! Maybe I'm better. *(She goes out.)*

AMETISTOV: *(Looking over the apartment.)* Voilà—It's paradise, isn't it, Count? Oh, cheer up! Why are you sitting there all hunched up like an old kneading tub?

ABOLYANINOV: What is that, exactly, a "kneading tub?"

AMETISTOV: I give up! You're the hardest man to have a simple chat with!…Well, so what do you think of our little apartment?

ABOLYANINOV: Very cozy. It reminds me of my former apartment…

AMETISTOV: Was it nice?

ABOLYANINOV: Very nice, but they took it away from me…

AMETISTOV: No!

ABOLYANINOV: Yes. Some big men with red beards walked in and threw me out…

AMETISTOV: Are such things possible? What a sad story!

ZOYA: *(Entering.)* Good evening, Pavlik! Why are you so pale! Come into the light so I can look at you…And there are circles under your eyes…

ABOLYANINOV: Oh, it's nothing…I've been sleeping too much.

ZOYA: Come sit with me until our guests arrive.

(She leaves with Abolyaninov. The doorbell rings. It's a signal: three longs, two shorts.)

AMETISTOV: It's about time!

(Manyushka runs to answer the door. Cherubim enters with a laundry bundle.)

Where the hell have you been?

CHERUBIM: I iron for Zoya—sure, sure.

AMETISTOV: The hell with the ironing. Did you bring the cocaine?

CHERUBIM: I bring.

AMETISTOV: Let's have it! *(He opens the laundry bundle and finds the cocaine.)* Look here, Mr. Mee-Wan-Tea, look me in the eye.

CHERUBIM: I look.

AMETISTOV: Tell me the truth, did you mix this with aspirin?

CHERUBIM: No mix!

AMETISTOV: I know you, you Chinese bandit! If you mixed it with anything, God will punish you! *(He snorts a pinch of it.)*

CHERUBIM: Punish—sure, sure.

AMETISTOV: Sure, sure? He'll smash you on the spot! He'll bang you on the top of the head and no more Chinaman! *Thou shalt not mix cocaine with aspirin!*...Ahhh!...No, this is fine. Well then, beloved son of the sub-Celestial Empire, it's time to get changed.

(Cherubim puts on a Chinese hat and silk jacket.)

There, that's more like it! But why in the world do you Chinamen cut off your braids? You'd be worth a lot more to me with a braid.

(The doorbell rings—Mymra's signal.)

Ah, ha! Good old Mymra, she's the first.

CHERUBIM: Mymra come! Mymra come!

AMETISTOV: Oh, no! Stop right there! Who do you think you are? She's not Mymra to you.

MYMRA: *(Coming in.)* Hello, Aleksander Tarasovich. Cherubimchik! *(Noticing the flowers set out by Ametistov and Manyushka.)* Oh, chrysanthemums! But they're my favorite flowers, I adore them! *(She sings.)*
"...And promise to bring me chrysanthemums,
When I am in my grave."

AMETISTOV: Hurry, Marya Nikiforovna, get dressed. It's late, and we have a big night ahead of us. We'll be showing the new gowns.

MYMRA: They're here? That's wonderful! *(She rushes off.)*

(Cherubim lights a Chinese incense burner, which begins to send out clouds of aromatic smoke.)

AMETISTOV: Don't overdo it, Cherubim.

CHERUBIM: No overdo.

(Cherubim runs off. The doorbell rings. Lizanka comes in.)

LIZANKA: My respects to the Mother Superior.

AMETISTOV: *Bon soir,* Lizanka. Go get changed—fly, fly! A very important guest is on his way.

LIZANKA: To see me?

AMETISTOV: Well...that's for him to say, of course.

LIZANKA: I've been feeling a little neglected lately.

(Lizanka disappears. The doorbell rings. Ametistov runs to the mirror and primps. Madame Ivanova enters. She is very beautiful and haughty.)

ACT II

AMETISTOV: Good evening, Madame Ivanova.

MADAME IVANOVA: Cigarette.

AMETISTOV: Manyushka! Cigarettes!

> *(Manyushka runs in and gives Madame Ivanova a cigarette. Pause.)*

> What's it like out there tonight? Cold, huh?

MADAME IVANOVA: Cold.

AMETISTOV: We have a surprise for you—the new collection is here from Paris.

MADAME IVANOVA: Good.

AMETISTOV: Such magnificent gowns! Absolutely delectable!

MADAME IVANOVA: Uh-huh.

AMETISTOV: You came on the trolley?

MADAME IVANOVA: Yes.

AMETISTOV: Was it crowded?

MADAME IVANOVA: Yes.

> *(Pause.)*

AMETISTOV: Your cigarette has gone out. Match?

MADAME IVANOVA: Thank you. *(She exits.)*

AMETISTOV: What a woman! You could spend your entire life with a woman like that and never get bored. Not like you, Manyushka, you little chatterbox.

(The doorbell is rung with authority.)

Now that's the ring of a Coordinating Director. What a bell-ringer! Let him in, Manyushka, then go get ready—Cherubim will take over!

CHERUBIM: *(Running in.)* Goos! Goos! *(He runs out again.)*

MANYUSHKA: Oh, my goodness! Goos! *(She runs to open the door.)*

AMETISTOV: Zoya! Zoya! Goos! Goos!

(Zoya enters in a beautiful gown.)

You greet him, it's time for me to disappear! *(He goes out.)*

(Goos enters.)

ZOYA: My dear Boris Semyonich, how delightful to see you!

GOOS: Hello, Zoya Denisovna! Hello!

ZOYA: Sit over here, it's more comfortable. Shame, shame, shame... what a bad boy you are!

GOOS: But this is unbelievable! All Moscow keeps telling me what a good boy I am, and you say I'm bad.

ZOYA: Moscow is a flatterer, Boris Semyonich. She bows down before her great men. But how can I flatter you—I'm only a seam-stress...You're a close friend, a neighbor, and you've never even paid us a visit. Shame on you.

GOOS: Believe me...I would have been here long ago, but I...

ZOYA: I'm teasing you...I know you must be up to your ears in work...   .

GOOS: Well, not all the way up to my ears, perhaps, but I'm very busy...I have meetings all morning, meetings all afternoon, meetings all evening. And at night...

ZOYA: More meetings?

GOOS: Insomnia.

ZOYA: You poor man, you'll wear yourself out.

GOOS: I already have.

ZOYA: You see? What you need is a little diversion.

GOOS: With a workload like mine, I don't even think about diversion. *(He notices the painting.)* Look at that! What a picture! What a master!

ZOYA: It's from the French school.

GOOS: What a school! That's what I call a school, all right! Would you consider selling it?

ZOYA: Would you like to buy it?

GOOS: I don't see why not. I love pictures. I just moved into a large apartment, you know, and my walls are bare...if you'll pardon the expression.

ZOYA: And you'd like to cover one bare wall with a naked woman? So that's the kind of boy you are!

GOOS: You're always so...intriguing.

ZOYA: Actually, I wasn't planning to sell the picture, but when I go abroad, I'll give it to you.

GOOS: Give it to me? Why?

ZOYA: Because you've done so much for me. Without you, I wouldn't even have a workshop.

GOOS: Don't mention it. Uh...that reminds me...I'm here partly because of the workshop. Now, this is just between you and me...I need a dress. From Paris. The latest thing, you know, whatever the rage is. For, say, two-fifty, three hundred rubles...

ZOYA: I see. A little present for somebody?

GOOS: Well...this is just between you and me.

ZOYA: Oh, you bad, bad boy! You're in love! Come on, admit it. You're in love?

GOOS: Just between you and me.

ZOYA: Don't worry, I won't tell your wife. Oh, you men!

GOOS: *(Looking back at the painting.)* That really is a great master!

ZOYA: Well, then I can arrange everything, on one condition: that this, too, is just between you and me. My manager will give you a private showing of our collection, and you can pick the dress you want. Then we'll have a little supper. Tonight you belong only to me, and I won't share you.

GOOS: *Merci.* So you even have a manager? Well, well, let's have a look at him.

ACT II

ZOYA: He'll be right with you. *(She slips away.)*

AMETISTOV: *(Appearing suddenly, in full evening dress.)* Quand on parle du soleil, on voit le rayon—which is to say, "Just mention the sun and it's already shining."

GOOS: Are you talking to me?

AMETISTOV: But of course, my dear Boris Semyonovich. Allow me to introduce myself—Ametistov!

GOOS: Goos.

AMETISTOV: I hear you're looking for a gown? Well, good for you, my dear Boris Semyonovich! We have the finest selection in Moscow. Cherubim!

(Cherubim appears.)

GOOS: But he's a Chinaman!

AMETISTOV: Precisely! A Chinaman, if that meets with your approval? Don't let it trouble you, my esteemed Boris Semyonich. He's a typical son of the sub-Celestial Empire, unique in only one thing: he's a paragon of honesty.

(Cherubim goes out.)

GOOS: But why a Chinaman?

AMETISTOV: Oh, most respected Boris Semyonich, he's my old and faithful servant, completely devoted to me. I brought him back from Shanghai, where I wandered for years collecting material.

GOOS: Amazing. Material for what?

AMETISTOV: ...For a comprehensive anthropological study. One day I'll tell you all my adventures, most profoundly revered Boris Semyonich, and you'll be sobbing, I guarantee it. Cherubim!

(Cherubim appears immediately with champagne.)

GOOS: Champagne, too? What a fine Citizen-Manager you are!

AMETISTOV: *Je pense!* When you work at *Paquin's*...you know, in *Paris*...you develop a certain sense of style.

GOOS: You worked in Paris?

AMETISTOV: *Mais oui,* my most amiable and obliging Boris Semyonich, for five years! You may go now, Cherubim.

(Cherubim disappears.)

GOOS: What a face! You know, if I believed in such things, I'd think he really was a cherub!

AMETISTOV: Yes, when you look at his face, you can almost hear the angels singing...To your health, your Highness! And the health of your Essential Metals Industries! Oo-rah! Oo-rah and oo-rah! Come on now, bottoms up! Don't insult the establishment!

GOOS: And what a remarkable establishment it is!

AMETISTOV: *Milles mercis!* So tell me...is she blonde or brunette?

GOOS: Who?

AMETISTOV: *Pardon, pardon.* That special someone...for whom the new *ensemble* is intended.

GOOS: Well...just between you and me...she's more a brunette.

AMETISTOV: Perfect! Here, have some more...*(He pours the champagne.)*...and if you'll please stand up for a moment...

GOOS: *(Rising.)* Yes?

AMETISTOV: *Merci...(He looks Goos over.)* Well, well...this elegant cutaway positively cries out for a light brunette.

GOOS: Yeah? And what if I take it off? Boy, this is strong champagne!

AMETISTOV: If you take it off...we can come up with the right brunette for whatever you're wearing. We'll astonish you!

GOOS: I'm already astonished.

AMETISTOV: Cherubim!

(Cherubim appears.)

Ask the maestro to step in, and call Mademoiselle Liza.

CHERUBIM: I go.

(Cherubim disappears. Abolyaninov enters.)

AMETISTOV: *Comte* Abolyaninov!

(Abolyaninov sits down at the piano.)

Make yourself comfortable, Boris Semyonich, my dear. Help yourself to the almonds. *(He claps his hands.)* Atelier!

(Abolyaninov begins to play something sad. The curtain opens on a lighted platform. Lizanka, in a gorgeous, low-cut gown, enacts a young lady shivering with cold. Cherubim stands at the side sprinkling handfuls of snow on her. Goos looks on in astonishment.)

Why are you crying, you poor little thing?

(Pause.)

Crucified by cocaine on the cold boulevards of Moscow…

(Lizanka expires beside a public trash receptacle.)

…your purple body will be covered by a shroud of mist.

(Lizanka suddenly comes back to life, jumps up, and dances wildly.)

Enfant terrible! Merci, mademoiselle.

LIZANKA: *(In a whisper.)* Shall I scram?

AMETISTOV: Yes, Lizanka. Scram.

(Lizanka disappears. Abolyaninov stops playing. Ametistov pulls the curtain closed.)

Well, my most admired Boris Semyonich, what did you think of that?

GOOS: Not bad at all…

AMETISTOV: More champagne?

GOOS: *Merci.* You're so refined…

AMETISTOV: Well, after all, Boris Semyonich, you're bound to pick up a thing or two, rubbing elbows at the Imperial Court.

GOOS: You were at the Imperial Court?

AMETISTOV: Oh, Boris Semyonich, if you only knew. One of these days, I'll reveal the mysteries of my birth, and you'll be flooded with tears.

GOOS: Terrific! Uh...don't you have a gown a little more...?

AMETISTOV: Covered?...

GOOS: No...uncovered!

AMETISTOV: Of course! I'm beginning to get a real sense of what you like, my most respected Boris Semyonich...Leave everything to me! *(He picks up a violin.) Atelier!*

(Again the curtain opens. Mymra, in a beautiful and fairly revealing gown, mimes feeding the pigeons, while Ametistov, accompanied by Abolyaninov, plays a Chopin nocturne.)

Careful, Marya Nikiforovna, don't bend over so far. The night is still young.

MYMRA: Don't tell me what to do!

AMETISTOV: *(Playing.)* Pick it up, *Mademoiselle Marie.*

(The music stops.)

Psst! Go!

MYMRA: *(As the curtain closes.)* Philistine!

AMETISTOV: *(Calling after her.) Vous êtes très aimable.* Well, my delightful Boris Semyonich, how about that? *Atelier!*

(Abolyaninov plays "The Moon Is Shining," and the curtain opens on Manyushka, dancing a Russian dance in a very revealing Russian costume. Ametistov plays along on the balalaika.)

CHERUBIM: *(Popping out, in a whisper.)* You dance only for me, Manooska! Nobody else…!

MANYUSHKA: You jealous devil, get away!

ABOLYANINOV: *(Bursting out.)* I'm playing the piano while the maid dances…What's happening to Moscow?

AMETISTOV: Psst, Manyushka! Get off the stage! Go serve supper, right this minute! *(The curtain closes. To Goos.)* Eh, bien?

GOOS: *(With enthusiasm.)* Atelier!

AMETISTOV: That's it, you great big beautiful Boris Semyonich, you've got it! *Atelier!*

(Abolyaninov launches into a passionate waltz. The curtain opens, and Madame Ivanova appears in a gown as revealing as the censors will allow.)

How do you like my little production now, Boris Semyonich?

(Ametistov jumps up on the stage and waltzes with Madame Ivanova. He pauses to call attention to her bare shoulders.)

Décolleté sur les bras!

(They dance. He pauses again, this time to run his fingers down her bare back.)

Décolleté…sur le dos!

(They dance. To her, quietly.)

To tell you the truth, Madame Ivanova, I'm a very unhappy man. All I dream about is Nice, being in Nice with the woman I love…where the rhododendrons bloom…

MADAME IVANOVA: *(Dancing.)* Chatterbox...

AMETISTOV: *(Stopping suddenly.)* And now—the man with your fate in his hands delivers you up to your destiny!

(He throws Madame Ivanova at the feet of Goos. The music stops abruptly.)

CHERUBIM: *(Popping out from behind the curtain and applauding.)* Production by Ametistov!

AMETISTOV: *(Modestly.)* Oh, come on now...come on...

(Cherubim disappears.)

So, my most exalted and sublime Boris Semyonich, how do you like the slashes in that dress?

GOOS: I don't know, Citizen-Manager. Where are they?

AMETISTOV: Show the *monsieur, Madame. Pardon, pardon. (He disappears.)*

MADAME IVANOVA: *(Stepping down from the atelier stage as a figure might step out of a painting.)* Would you like to see my slashes, *Monsieur...?*

GOOS: I'd be so grateful, from the bottom of my heart...

MADAME IVANOVA: *(Suddenly sitting on his lap.)* Stop it—what are you doing? You bold thing. Don't you dare hold me so tight!

GOOS: Who says I'm holding you?!

MADAME IVANOVA: You're so impetuous! Like a Zulu.

GOOS: You flatter me. I've never even been to Africa.

MADAME IVANOVA: Maybe you've read about it. *(She kisses him.)* No, what are you doing? Oh, you're so bold, so reckless! Don't touch me, someone might come in! But you know, I like men who won't take no for an answer. *(She kisses him again.)* I'm lost!

AMETISTOV: *(Suddenly appearing.)* Pardon.

MADAME IVANOVA: Oh! *(She disappears.)*

GOOS: *(In a frenzy.)* Atelier!!

AMETISTOV: *Pardon, pardon. Entracte.* Intermission.

CURTAIN

ACT III

SCENE ONE
Zoya's Apartment. Three Days Later.

(A gray day. The vases are filled with flowers. Aliluya is whispering ominously to Ametistov, who is in formal evening wear.)

AMETISTOV: And what malicious viper told you that?

ALILUYA: What viper? People talk, that's all! They say there's a lot of traffic in this apartment.

AMETISTOV: Please explain to me, my respected Lord Mayor of Sadovaya Street, how we can have a workshop without traffic?

ALILUYA: A workshop with fox-trots? Night after night? Look at it from my point of view…

AMETISTOV: Your point of view?…Ah, yes, of course! Zoya Denisovna still owes you twenty rubles, doesn't she?…for the electricity.

ALILUYA: Thirty!

AMETISTOV: Twenty-five?

ALILUYA: No, thirty!

AMETISTOV: If you say it's thirty, it's thirty. Here.

ALILUYA: I'll send a receipt tomorrow.

AMETISTOV: Forget it, comrade. Who needs all that red tape…Hic! …Damn it!

ALILUYA: You still have the hiccups? Someone must be thinking of you.

AMETISTOV: I wonder who?

ALILUYA: …Listen, Aleksander Tarasovich, you're attracting too much attention! I'm begging you, go easy on the fox-trots for a while…you're not expecting company again tonight, are you?

AMETISTOV: Only a few friends—a little name-day celebration.

ALILUYA: Well, I'd better be on my way. Good-bye now. *(He offers to shake hands.)*

AMETISTOV: Handshakes have been abolished, comrade! *(He chuckles.)* Just a little joke. *Revoir.*

(Aliluya goes out.)

I've seen a lot of bribe takers in my life, but Aliluya is a revelation. Hic! Damn it! Maybe I overdid it with that herring…

(Abolyaninov, also dressed for the party, drifts in like a shadow, looking sad.)

Hic! *Pardon!*

(The telephone rings.)

Cherubim! Telephone!

(Cherubim enters and answers the phone.)

CHERUBIM: Hello, hello…Goos? Here Goos! *(He goes out.)*

AMETISTOV: *(Picking up the phone.)* Comrade Goos?…Felicitations,

Boris Semyonich, how are you?...Oh, we're as busy as little bees!...Yes, of course we're expecting you tonight...It's a perfect night for it!...Around ten o'clock, then...Hic!...*Pardon...*I'll bet your ears were burning, we've been talking about you...Oh, yes, she does, she said, "When am I going to see that Assyrian profile again?"...What?...No, no, no, secret, secret, secret! We have a big surprise for you, Boris Semyonich...My warmest regards! Good-bye. *(He hangs up.)* Hic!

ABOLYANINOV: That Goos is a vulgar fellow, don't you think, exceedingly vulgar?

AMETISTOV: I most certainly do not. How can you call a man who earns five thousand rubles a month vulgar? Hic!...Somebody *is* thinking about me...Who, I wonder? Who wants me?...No, I have the utmost respect for Goos...After all, Goos isn't the one who trudges around Moscow all day, wearing out his shoes.

ABOLYANINOV: Pardon me, Monsieur Ametistov, but I do not "trudge." I walk.

AMETISTOV: Here we go again. Don't be so sensitive! All right, let's say you walk. But Goos rides around in a car. You're cooped up in one little room—*pardon, pardon*—perhaps the phrase "cooped up" is not acceptable in high society—let's say you're "in residence" in one little room. Goos has seven. You have to pound the piano—*pardon, pardon*—I mean, "tickle the ivories," for a measly one hundred rubles a month. Goos gets five thousand. You have to sit and play—and Goos gets to dance.

ABOLYANINOV: That's because this regime has made it impossible for decent people to survive.

AMETISTOV: *Pardon, pardon!* Decent people can survive anything. I'm a decent person, and I'm surviving. Remember, papa, when I got here, I didn't even have a good pair of trousers...

ABOLYANINOV: Pardon me, what kind of "papa" am I to you, exactly?

AMETISTOV: Oh, don't be such a prig! "Papa." It's just my way of…men of our class always…hic!

ABOLYANINOV: Excuse me, but are you really an aristocrat?

AMETISTOV: What a silly question! Can't you tell?…hic!…Damn it!

ABOLYANINOV: I've never heard of the Ametistovs.

AMETISTOV: Really? Well, it's a name known to every single person in the Penza province! Oh, *signor!* If you only knew what I had to endure at the hands of the Bolsheviks, your hair would stand on end…First they looted the estate, then they put my chateau to the torch…

ABOLYANINOV: Where, exactly, was this chateau?

AMETISTOV: Mine? You're asking about my chateau?

ABOLYANINOV: Yes. The one they put to the torch…

AMETISTOV: Oh, that one…in, uh…oh, I don't even want to think about it—it's still too painful! White columns…yes, it's all coming back to me. *Un, deux, trois…vier, fünf, sechs…*seven. Yes, seven huge columns, each more beautiful than the last. Oh, why go on about it? And all my cattle! With their pedigrees! And my brickworks!

ABOLYANINOV: My aunt, Varvara Nikolayevna, had a wonderful stable…

AMETISTOV: Your Aunt Varvara! What about me? I had a stable too, and it was great!…What's the matter with you today, anyway? Cheer up, papasha.

ABOLYANINOV: So many memories are coming back to me...I had a horse...his name was Pharaoh...Oh, I sympathize with you...

AMETISTOV: Who wouldn't?

ABOLYANINOV: I'm so sad...

AMETISTOV: Me, too! I wonder why? Maybe I'm having some kind of premonition...The best cure for sadness is cards!

ABOLYANINOV: I don't like cards...I like horses...Pharaoh. In 1913, in Petersburg, he won the *Grand prix*...The jockey was a little Englishman...I can't remember his name..."They remind me"...

(We hear a voice raised in song: "They remind me...")

...he had a red jacket with yellow sleeves, and a black bandolier! Pharaoh!

AMETISTOV: Faro! What a game!...The dealer slowly turns up the corner of the card, and you, papa, you break out in a cold sweat. And all of a sudden, whap!—the card lies there on the table as if it has been mowed down by a scythe, and you've got yourself a winner!...Maybe it's Aliluya, maybe he's put me in this mood...My God, I have to get out of here!

ABOLYANINOV: Yes, I, too, as soon as possible. I can't stand this any longer.

AMETISTOV: Hang on, little brother. In three months we'll be on our way to Nice! Say, Count, have you ever been to Nice!

ABOLYANINOV: Many times.

AMETISTOV: Oh...Me, too. In early childhood. What memories! My

73

late mother used to take me there. From our chateau. Two governesses came along. And that's not counting the nanny. My hair was so curly in those days!...Are there cardsharps in Monte Carlo, I wonder? There probably are.

ABOLYANINOV: I don't know... *(Sadly.)*...I don't know anything...

AMETISTOV: You really are sad, aren't you? Oh, Count, you're such a delicate bloom. Listen, dear colleague, before Zoyechka gets back, let's sneak away to the "New Bavaria" and have a couple of beers. What do you say? Come on. Some doctors actually even prescribe beer for melancholy.

ABOLYANINOV: You astonish me! Beer halls are so common! Filthy, disgusting...

AMETISTOV: You obviously haven't seen the lobsters they got in yesterday at the "New Bavaria!" Each lobster—and I'm not exaggerating—the size of a guitar! Let's go, papachka!

ABOLYANINOV: All right, let's go.

AMETISTOV: Good for you! Cherubim!

(Cherubim appears.)

Listen, when Zoya Denisovna gets home, tell her the Count and I stepped around the corner for a moment to the Tretyakov Gallery. We'll be right back. Did you get that?

CHERUBIM: Sure, sure—I get.

AMETISTOV: I can see by your eyes you didn't get a thing. Tell her we'll be back in twenty minutes. Put the champagne on ice, and also the vodka, and set out the red wine...In a word, my dear

Major-Domo of the Yellow Race, I leave the apartment in your capable hands and under your complete authority. Well, Count, *allez-vous-en!* To the "New Bavaria!" Lobsters, *en garde!*

(Ametistov and Abolyaninov go out.)

CHERUBIM: Manooska! They go!

MANYUSHKA: *(Running in and kissing him.)* What makes me like you so much? You're the color of a baby orange, but I still feel so close to you! Hey…you Chinese aren't Lutherans, are you?

CHERUBIM: Lutheran. Sure, sure—wash clothes…Wait, Manooska. Important business! We go soon. We go Shanghai.

MANYUSHKA: Shanghai? Who's going to Shanghai!

CHERUBIM: You go!

MANYUSHKA: "You go!" Since when do you give the orders? Did we get married?

CHERUBIM: I marry you Shanghai, Manooska.

MANYUSHKA: You have to ask me first. Did I promise? I never put anything in writing!

CHERUBIM: Oh! Maybe you like marry Gan-Tsa-Lin?

MANYUSHKA: Why shouldn't I? I can do whatever I like. Don't pop your Chinese eyes at me, I'm not afraid of you.

CHERUBIM: You marry Gan-Tsa-Lin?!

MANYUSHKA: Calm down, calm down!

CHERUBIM: *(Becoming terrible.)* Gan-Tsa-Lin?!

MANYUSHKA: Hey, hey, what's the matter with you?

(Cherubim whips out his knife and grabs her by the throat.)

CHERUBIM: Cut you, kill you!

(He chokes her.)

Say now, you say true! You kiss Gan-Tsa-Lin?

MANYUSHKA: Let go! Stop! Stop, my angel!…Oh, Father in Heaven, in her hour of need, remember your servant, Maria…

CHERUBIM: You kiss? You kiss Gan-Tsa-Lin?

MANYUSHKA: Cherubimchik, precious angel…*(She holds up one finger.)*…only once, one little kiss, I swear it! Have mercy on me, I'm an orphan…

CHERUBIM: *(Putting his knife away.)* You no marry Gan-Tsa-Lin?

MANYUSHKA: No, no, no…

CHERUBIM: You marry me?

MANYUSHKA: No, no, no…yes, yes, yes! What are you doing to me?!

CHERUBIM: I make proposal.

MANYUSHKA: Some proposal. A real Shanghai proposal—at the point of a knife! You're a bandit, Cherubim!

CHERUBIM: No…I no bandit!…Was so sad, Manooska. Everyone chase me…want put me prison for cocaine…Gan-Tsa-Lin, he bandit...sure, sure. I wash clothes, deliver laundry, cocaine...He take money, take all money, give me forty kopeck...Now, I live nice apartment...Was so cold, Manooska...Moscow too cold for Chinaman, cannot live Moscow...Chinaman need live Shanghai. I love you, Manooska, love you so much. We have own business Shanghai, sell opium. Be so happy...You have baby, Chinese baby—sure, sure—six, eight, ten!

MANYUSHKA: Ten? I'll hang myself...

CHERUBIM: Everybody want hang self, Moscow. Shanghai, Chinese happy. Get ready now, take all, all, we go soon...I know way get many rubles...

MANYUSHKA: What way? Oh, Cherubimka, what are you talking about? You're scaring me!

(The doorbell rings.)

Quick! Go to the kitchen!

(Cherubim runs out. She answers the door.)

Oh, dear lord! My God!

GAN-TSA-LIN: Hello, Manooska!

MANYUSHKA: Oh, Gasoline, go away...

GAN-TSA-LIN: No! Why go? No go! Alone, Manooska? I come say propose you.

MANYUSHKA: Propose me?

GAN-TSA-LIN: Today Sunday! Laundry close.

MANYUSHKA: What's gotten into you, Gasoline? Go away!

GAN-TSA-LIN: No go! Why go? What you say me all long time? You love me! You no love me? Cheat Gan-Tsa-Lin?!

MANYUSHKA: That's not true! Why are you acting like this? I'll call Zoya Denisovna...

GAN-TSA-LIN: You lie. She not home. You lie all time, Manooska, sure, sure—but...I love you!

MANYUSHKA: Do you have a knife? Tell me right now, do you have a knife?

GAN-TSA-LIN: I have knife! Propose you!

CHERUBIM: *(Appearing suddenly.)* You propose who?

GAN-TSA-LIN: Ah-ha! Here my assistant! Oh-ho, you son-of-bitch!

CHERUBIM: You go way! Go way from apartment! This my apartment...me and Zoyka!

MANYUSHKA: Oh, what's going to happen?

GAN-TSA-LIN: You apartment? You bandit, now you steal apartment! You poor dog I take you in! You go way!...I come say propose Manooska.

CHERUBIM: Too late! She my wife, she love me!

GAN-TSA-LIN: You lie! She my wife, she love me! *(He takes out his knife.)*

MANYUSHKA: He's lying, Cherubimchik, lying, lying! One little kiss, that's all!

ACT III

CHERUBIM: Get out my apartment!

GAN-TSA-LIN: You get out! I go police. Tell what kind Chinese bandit you!

CHERUBIM: *(Hissing.)* Police!

(Gan-Tsa-Lin hisses back. They hiss at each other.)

MANYUSHKA: Dear little bunnies, don't kill each other, you devils!

(Cherubim whips out his knife and lunges at Gan-Tsa-Lin.)

CHERUBIM: A-a-a-a!…

MANYUSHKA: Help! Help! Help!

(Gan-Tsa-Lin turns and runs to the wardrobe, opens it, jumps in, and closes the door behind him. Cherubim follows, brandishing his knife. The doorbell rings.)

Thank God! Throw down your knife, you vicious devil.

(Doorbell.)

They're after you! And they'll send you to Siberia!

(Doorbell.)

CHERUBIM: I cut him pieces! *(He hisses.)*

MANYUSHKA: Oh, stop that hissing! And hide behind the curtain!

(Cherubim locks the wardrobe, puts the key in his pocket, and hides behind the curtain. Manyushka opens the front door and Tubby comes in, followed by Vanyichka. They wear ordinary street clothes

79

*and carry briefcases. Vanyichka wears gold-rim glasses and the full
beard of an old professor.)*

Yes, comrade? How can I help you?

TUBBY: Greetings, comrade! We heard someone calling for help. It
wasn't you, was it?

MANYUSHKA: What are you talking about? I was singing.

TUBBY: You have a big voice, comrade.

MANYUSHKA: What can I do for you, comrades?

TUBBY: Well, comrade, we've been sent by the People's Commissariat
of Education to take a look at this workshop.

MANYUSHKA: Sorry, the director's not here. No classes today—it's
Sunday.

TUBBY: And who are you?

MANYUSHKA: I'm a student model.

TUBBY: I guess you'll have to show us around, then. We don't want to
make two trips.

MANYUSHKA: Well…I'll be glad to.

TUBBY: So…what goes on in here?

MANYUSHKA: This is the fitting room.

TUBBY: *(He points to the mannequins.)* What are those things? You
model the clothes on them, right?

MANYUSHKA: They're mannequins. Of course, that's what they're for.

TUBBY: Then what are models for?

MANYUSHKA: Well...when you have to adjust the clothes for movement, you put them on a student-model.

TUBBY: Uh-huh...You make things only for ladies, then?

MANYUSHKA: Ladies? We make clothes for women—work clothes for the proletariat.

(Tubby pulls open the curtain behind which Cherubim stands motionless, with an iron in his hand.)

TUBBY: Here's a funny mannequin, a Chinaman!

MANYUSHKA: They send him over from the laundry...to iron skirts and things...

TUBBY: Uh-huh...Go ahead, iron, iron! Don't let us stop you.

(Cherubim licks his finger, tests the temperature of the iron, and goes off with it.)

Well, well, well! Who actually resides on the premises?

MANYUSHKA: Our director, Comrade Peltz, and our manager, Aleksander Tarasovich Ametistov.

TUBBY: What a lovely name...Anyone else?

MANYUSHKA: Just me.

TUBBY: And who are you, comrade? Tell us a little something about yourself?

MANYUSHKA: Well, my papa was a peasant.

TUBBY: He was, was he? And what is he now?

MANYUSHKA: He's dead.

TUBBY: Sorry…How about your mother?

MANYUSHKA: Oh, she's a worker.

TUBBY: Where does she work?

MANYUSHKA: In the market in Tambov. She has a stall.

TUBBY: Good for her! Well, dear comrade, show me the rest of the apartment.

MANYUSHKA: Of course. This way, please. This is our small fitting room…

(As Manyushka and Tubby go into the mythical being's room, Vanyichka sets rapidly to work. He gives the room a once-over, inspects the furniture, looks in drawers, etc. He pulls open the curtain and comes upon the painting of the nude.)

VANYICHKA: Oh, ho! Here's a subject for further investigation!

(He takes out a skeleton key, unlocks the wardrobe, and opens the door. Gan-Tsa-Lin crouches inside with a knife in his hand. Vanyichka jumps back in alarm.)

GAN-TSA-LIN: *(Softly.)* Help me!

VANYICHKA: Another one? Wherever you look, there's a Chinaman! What are you doing in there?

GAN-TSA-LIN: *(Whispering.)* I sit!

VANYICHKA: *(Also whispering.)* But why?

GAN-TSA-LIN: *(Near tears.)* I hide—sure, sure. He bandit! Want cut me pieces! Help me!

VANYICHKA: Relax, you're safe now. *(Whispering.)* What are you doing here, anyway?

GAN-TSA-LIN: I come say propose maid, and he try kill me. Devil bandit! Oh, he bring opium. Smoke opium here. Dance, dance, everybody dance...He bandit! You get him! *(He pops out of the wardrobe and darts out the door.)*

VANYICHKA: So that's what goes on here.

(Vanyichka closes the wardrobe and locks it again. Tubby and Manyushka return.)

TUBBY: Well, everything is in order. There's plenty of light, good ventilation—it's quite a workshop!

VANYICHKA: Isn't that the truth? Tell me, dear comrade, what's in this wardrobe?

MANYUSHKA: In there?...What's in there?...Oh, all sorts of rags and remnants. I don't have the key. Our director has it.

VANYICHKA: Don't worry about it. We'll look at it some other time.

TUBBY: Well, comrade model, you may tell your director that a delegation from the People's Commissariat of Education inspected the workshop and found everything in perfect order. She deserves a citation.

VANYICHKA: Isn't that the truth?

(They go out through the hallway. Manyushka closes the door after them.)

CHERUBIM: *(Leaping out like a typhoon, brandishing his knife.)* Ahhh! They go? *(He races to the wardrobe.)* So, Gan-Tsa-Lin, you say police get me? I get you!

MANYUSHKA: Help! Devil! Help! Devil!

(Cherubim throws open the wardrobe and stands in amazement.)

CHERUBIM: Son-of-bitch!…He must have key!

(Blackout.)

SCENE TWO
Headquarters. Later That Day.

(Out of the darkness a mysterious lamp with a green shade lights up, revealing a huge desk with many telephones.)

COMRADE PESTRUKHIN: And then what?

TUBBY: At that point…according to Vanyichka, he jumped up and ran out the door. We can pick him up later…

COMRADE PESTRUKHIN: But he'll tip them off—he'll start a panic.

TUBBY: He doesn't know anything…As for the one behind the curtain…Vanyichka thinks he may have something going with the maid.

COMRADE PESTRUKHIN: What's her story…just a maid, right?

TUBBY: Oh, no! She's a clever little devil! A fox-trot queen!

COMRADE PESTRUKHIN: Vanyichka!

TUBBY: Oh, Vanya!!

VANYICHKA: *(Walking in.)* Vanyichka? Who's Vanyichka? I was Vanyichka for forty years, and now look at me! *(He pulls off his beard and glasses.)* I should take this beard and stuff it down his throat. A beard is supposed to put people at their ease—inspire trust! I told him to give me a trim little beard like a doctor or a commissar, you know what I mean, something suitable for a representative of the People's Commissariat of Education and he gives me this preposterous cliché of our outmoded class system. What a bumbler! Amateurs like that should be thrown on the dust heap!

COMRADE PESTRUKHIN: Everything worked out, so forget it.

VANYICHKA: What kind of logic is that? We're just lucky we got the maid. A real pro like Ametistov would have known right away these are no Lunacharsky whiskers.

COMRADE PESTRUKHIN: All right. *(He picks up a telephone.)* B-V-1-5. Get me Operations…Lbov? What in the hell is going on down there in the beard department?…What do you mean, nothing? Your boys fixed up one of our boys today and gave him a ridiculous professor's beard. Who the hell do you think you are, the Moscow Art Theater?

VANYICHKA: Ask him about the warts!

COMRADE PESTRUKHIN: And another thing…you sent out a landlord today without warts!…Then get some! *(He hangs up.)*

VANYICHKA: Imagine! A landlord without warts! Amateurs!

COMRADE PESTRUKHIN: All right, all right, give it a rest. The second Chinaman—you know him?

VANYICHKA: Nope.

COMRADE PESTRUKHIN: What was he doing there?

VANYICHKA: Love.

COMRADE PESTRUKHIN: The maid again?

VANYICHKA: Bull's-eye.

COMRADE PESTRUKHIN: Deedle deedle dum, deedle dum. *(He picks up the phone.)* 6-1-5-double 0. Comrade Kalancheyev?…It's me…You don't recognize my voice? Me!…That's right!…Well, we had some of our boys check out that apartment, as you requested. Did you find out if she has a permit?…Oh, she does, does she? Huh! All right, *merci.* So long. *(He hangs up.)*

TUBBY: Open and shut.

COMRADE PESTRUKHIN: Deedle deedle dum, deedle dum. So, who have we got?

TUBBY: First, Zoyka. Next, Abolyaninov. Then, Ametistov, the maid…the Chinamen…

COMRADE PESTRUKHIN: *(Trying to write it all down.)* Hold on, hold on. "…the Chinamen."

TUBBY: …the guy who's away on business—a mythical being.

COMRADE PESTRUKHIN: He doesn't exist?

VANYICHKA: Isn't that the truth?

COMRADE PESTRUKHIN: So what's her game?

VANYICHKA: Space allocation…

COMRADE PESTRUKHIN: Anybody else involved?

TUBBY: Models. Guests at the name-day parties.

COMRADE PESTRUKHIN: We'll get to them. Who's the Apartment House Chairman?

TUBBY: Aliluya, Anisim Zotikovich.

COMRADE PESTRUKHIN: Deedle deedle dum, deedle dum.

(He rings a bell and a little lighted window appears in the wall.)

Get me the file on Aliluya, Anisim Zotikovich.

VOICE: *(Through the window.)* Here we are. Aliluya, Anisim Zotikovich. Age: forty-two. Apartment House Committee Chairman since 1922. Married, but cheats. No bank account. Drinks. Dark hair. Suspected of taking bribes. Medium height. Wants to join the Party. Applied for membership.

COMRADE PESTRUKHIN: Photograph?

VOICE: Yes, indeed. Here's one from 1922. He's addressing the Apartment House Committee on the topic of international affairs.

(The photograph of Aliluya appears on a screen.)

TUBBY: Perfect casting.

VANYICHKA: Isn't that the truth?

COMRADE PESTRUKHIN: Let's go on.

(The photograph of Aliluya disappears.)

Get me Abolyaninov.

TUBBY: Pavel Fyodorovich.

VOICE: Here we are. Abolyaninov, Pavel Fyodorovich. Age: thirty-five. Former Count. Long-term relationship with Zoya Denisovna Peltz, resident of Number 10 Sadovaya Street. Addict.

COMRADE PESTRUKHIN: Cocaine?

VOICE: Morphine.

COMRADE PESTRUKHIN: Counter-revolutionary?

VOICE: Non-active.

COMRADE PESTRUKHIN: What else?

VOICE: Hair: blond.

COMRADE PESTRUKHIN: Photograph?

(A photograph of Abolyaninov appears on the screen.)

Let's go on.

(The photograph disappears.)

Now for the Chinamen. Get me the China Section. Names?

ACT III

VANYICHKA: Unknown.

COMRADE PESTRUKHIN: How can that be, Vanyichka?

VANYICHKA: Well, Comrade Pestrukhin, they're not stupid. The one behind the curtain turned, and all I got was a side view. Their profiles are exactly alike, like kopecks. The bastards!

COMRADE PESTRUKHIN: Deedle deedle dum, deedle dum.

VOICE: *(Through the window.)* Here we are…the China Section.

COMRADE PESTRUKHIN: Start with laundrymen.

(One after the other, photographs of Chinese laundrymen appear on the screen.)

VANYICHKA: *(After each one.)* Next…next…next…

(The images disappear.)

COMRADE PESTRUKHIN: Try opium dealers.

VOICE: Right. Here you go.

(Other images are projected. The fifth is Gan-Tsa-Lin.)

VANYICHKA: Hold it! That's him!

COMRADE PESTRUKHIN: The guy in the wardrobe?

VANYICHKA: Absolutely!

COMRADE PESTRUKHIN: Read the file.

VOICE: Gan-Tsa-Lin, alias "Gasoline." Shanghai laundry—"The Happy Housewife"—on Samoteka Street. Age: forty. First arrest, 1920: possession of morphine. Currently under surveillance. Involved with Zoya Peltz's maid, Marya Garbatova.

VANYICHKA: Well, what do you know!

COMRADE PESTRUKHIN: Let's go on.

(On the screen, more images of Chinese men. The third is Cherubim.)

VANYICHKA: Stop, stop!

COMRADE PESTRUKHIN: File.

VOICE: Tsen-Tsin-Poh, alias "Cherubim." Age: twenty-eight. First arrest, April, 1920: possession of morphine. Second arrest, October, 1920: theft of linens from attic of the editor of "Executive Committee Bulletin." Sentence: six months in Butyrski Castle. Third arrest, sale of opium. Fourth arrest, sale of morphine. In 1922, convicted on charge of assault with Finnish knife. Sent back to Butyrski Castle. Disappeared end of 1922, reappeared early 1923, working in "The Happy Housewife," Gan-Tsa-Lin's laundry. Present whereabouts unknown.

TUBBY: Not for long.

COMRADE PESTRUKHIN: Let's go on. Go to Ametistov.

TUBBY: Aleksander Tarasovich.

VOICE: …No current file.

COMRADE PESTRUKHIN: Archives!

ACT III

VOICE: Right, archives…Here we are. Ametistov, Aleksander Tarasovich. Petersburg petty bourgeois. Age: thirty-five. Arrived Moscow 1917. Passed himself off as former hussar and set up gambling operation in "The Rose of the East" hotel on Tverskaya Street. Caught pulling fifth jack from under the table, subsequently taken for treatment to Soldatenkoffskaya Hospital. On release, went to work for hospital supply room. Attempted to requisition alcohol in the amount of five bucketfuls to sterilize instruments. Dismissed. End of 1917, departed for provinces.

COMRADE PESTRUKHIN: Place of residence?

VOICE: Since 25 May, has been living at Number 10 Sadovaya Street in apartment of Zoya Denisovna Peltz. Position: manager of needlecraft school and workshop.

COMRADE PESTRUKHIN: Photograph?

VOICE: Not available.

TUBBY: We'll get one tomorrow! Well, Comrade Pestrukhin, quite a collection, huh?

COMRADE PESTRUKHIN: Deedle deedle dum, deedle dum. How many times did she celebrate St. Zoya's day in August?

TUBBY: Three.

COMRADE PESTRUKHIN: So what do we do now?

TUBBY: We must be ever vigilant!

COMRADE PESTRUKHIN: And do what? That's the question.

(He rings three times. The window closes. Darkness. The mysterious green lamp glows.)

TUBBY: Well…it's a complicated business…

COMRADE PESTRUKHIN: Deedle deedle dum, deedle dum . . . Vanyichka!

VANYICHKA: Yes?

COMRADE PESTRUKHIN: What do you think?

VANYICHKA: Me? *(He considers.)* Very simple. You know that bumbler in operations—devil take him—well…he's got three tuxedos…

COMRADE PESTRUKHIN: You have a brain of gold, Vanyichka! *(He reaches for the phone.)*

TUBBY: There's no brain like it in all of Moscow!

(The lights begin to fade.)

COMRADE PESTRUKHIN: *(In the dark.)* Lbov?…We need your tuxedos!…Right!

(Darkness.)

SCENE THREE
The Apartment.

(Night. In the darkness, we hear a guitar and the sound of clinking glasses. The lights come up on a big, noisy party, which has spilled into the other rooms, including that of the mythical being, now the "salon." Champagne, flowers. In the background, the mannequins

stand smiling: we can't tell if they are dead or alive. Lizanka stands on a table, singing, to the accompaniment of Ametistov's guitar. The Poet and Mr. Robber look on.)

LIZANKA: *(Singing.)*
> "Why, oh, why do I love you,
> My little Communist so true?
> And why, non-Party suitor, do
> I always scorn and torture you."

AMETISTOV: *(Chanting.)* "And one more time, and once again, and oh, my darling, once again!"

THE POET: *Brava,* Lizanka!

MR. ROBBER: Bravo! Bravo! "And one more time!"

AMETISTOV: *(At the top of his voice, in a chromatic scale.)* More-more-more-more-more!

(Zoya enters from the salon in a dazzling gown. Behind her, roars of laughter and the sound of breaking glass.)

ZOYA: Who needs more champagne? Don't neglect our guests, Aleksander Tarasich!

AMETISTOV: Not for the world! Any guest of this establishment will be coddled and pampered and given everything his little heart desires! Cherubim!

(A curtain opens on Cherubim's alcove. A Chinese paper lantern has helped transform it into an opium den. Cherubim sits motionless, wearing his exotic costume. He looks like an idol made of stone. Behind him sits The Smoker in a rocking chair.)

THE SMOKER: *(Moaning.)* Nirvana…

CHERUBIM: *(Coming out of his alcove, mysterious and magnificent.)* What?

AMETISTOV: Champagne!

(Cherubim goes out.)

LIZANKA: *(Singing.)*
"I'll dig my darling up again
And bathe and dress him up again…"

AMETISTOV: *(Singing.)*
"And plant him in the ground again!"

THE POET: *Brava*, Lizanka!

MR. ROBBER: *(Simultaneously.)* Encore!

(They applaud. Cherubim returns, serves the champagne, and goes back to his alcove, closing the curtain behind him. As Zoya returns to the salon, there is another surge of noise. We hear the muffled howling of The Stiff and the laughter of Mymra and Madame Ivanova.)

ZOYA: *(Off.)* Ladies and gentlemen, what's going on in here? *(She closes the door behind her.)*

THE POET: Lizanka, Lizanka! I don't have the words to convey to you my…my…how shall I put it?…the depth of my admiration. Here are my poems. Read them! Then you will know the inmost secrets of my soul.

AMETISTOV: Bravo, bravo!

LIZANKA: *Merci. (She tucks the little book in her stocking.)*

MR. ROBBER: Kiss me, Lizanka!

THE POET: No, me! Kiss me!

MR. ROBBER: Leave her alone, young man!

THE POET: Aren't my poems worth a kiss, Lizanka?

AMETISTOV: *Pardon, pardon.* Can there be any doubt?

MR. ROBBER: Lizanka, get rid of this poet! Go away, young man—you're a pest!

THE POET: I beg your pardon! I have as much right to be here as you do! *(He is clearly drunk.)*

AMETISTOV: Forgive me, *mille pardons.* Lizanka's kiss is so enchanting, so sublime, that a rivalry cannot be avoided. You can't imagine how many rich and famous men have begged for Lizanka's kiss, on bended knee…

LIZANKA: *(Also drunk.)* And gotten it!

AMETISTOV: *Pardon, pardon.*

(In the salon, Abolyaninov plays a fox-trot on the grand piano, and the guests begin to dance.)

Pardon, pardon. I kissed her once myself! It was fabulous! It took me two months to stop sobbing…Oh, mademoiselle, *pardon!*

MR. ROBBER: I'm waiting, Lizanka!

THE POET: What about me? This big dodo in a pince-nez...

MR. ROBBER: Be careful, young man.

(Ametistov jumps up on the table, lights a lamp above Lizanka, and arranges her in a classic pose.)

AMETISTOV: Come away with me to the old slave market in Algiers or Baghdad! Ladies and gentlemen, in response to an over-whelming public demand, we will now auction Lizanka's kiss! We'll start with a bid of five...rubles!

MR. ROBBER: Six!

AMETISTOV: Six! We have a bid of six! Six—once...

LIZANKA: "...again and once again!"

AMETISTOV: Six—twice! *(He produces a gavel and pounds it.)*

THE POET: Seven rubles!

AMETISTOV: Seven rubles from the gentleman by the piano! Thank you seven times!

LIZANKA: "More-more-more-more-more!"

MR. ROBBER: Eight!

THE POET: Nine!

AMETISTOV: Terrific. Nine. We have nine.

(The alcove curtain opens and The Smoker leans out.)

THE SMOKER: *(With an eerie laugh.)* Ten.

ACT III

AMETISTOV: Well, thank you. From the alcove—ten.

THE SMOKER: Eleven.

AMETISTOV: You're enchanting. Eleven—once. Eleven—twice.

MR. ROBBER: I'm still bidding.

ZOYA: *(Returning suddenly.)* Only eleven rubles for Lizanka's kiss? Shame on you, gentlemen! I'll bid fifteen.

AMETISTOV: *Grand merci!* The house takes the lead! The house will not yield! Fifteen—once!...Fifteen—twice!...

(Zoya disappears. Offstage, the fox-trot continues.)

MR. ROBBER: I'm still bidding.

THE SMOKER: Sixteen, seventeen, eighteen, and nineteen, and twenty... "and one more time"...

LIZANKA: *(Joining in.)* "...time, and once again, and oh my darling, once again!"

AMETISTOV: The alcove pulls ahead. Twenty rubles from the alcove. Twenty rubles—once. Twenty rubles—twice...

MR. ROBBER: I give up.

AMETISTOV: They're giving up over there. The gentleman in the alcove is in the lead. Oh, how I envy you. Twenty rubles—twice...

THE POET: Oh, Lizanka! Lizanka, I am losing you! Read my book!

AMETISTOV: Twenty rubles—three times. Sold! Congratulations, you lucky man!

(The Smoker pulls out his wallet. Zoya reappears, as if by magic, and collects the two ten-ruble notes. She gives one to Lizanka, who tucks it in her stocking. Meanwhile, The Smoker clambers onto the table and puckers up, stretching his lips toward Lizanka.)

THE SMOKER: *(Pulling away.)* Oh, no! But I thought you were a boy...*(He goes back to the alcove.)* You can have my kiss.

THE POET: Me? Lizanka, he gave me your kiss!

MR. ROBBER: You feed on leftovers, young man. *(He goes into the salon.)*

AMETISTOV: *(With equanimity.)* Pardon, pardon. Don't insult the establishment!

(Ametistov disappears into the salon, leaving the door open. The foxtrot becomes somehow wilder. We hear peals of laughter, with more incomprehensible howling from The Stiff. The Foxtrotter sweeps on, with Madame Ivanova.)

THE FOXTROTTER: You dance divinely, my dear!
(Singing.)
    la-LA-la-la,
    la-LA-la...

MADAME IVANOVA: Your profile is Greek.

(Lizanka glides by, fox-trotting with The Poet.)

THE POET: There is something diabolical in this fox-trot, Lizanka, can't you feel it?—a crescendo of endless torment.

LIZANKA: *(Singing.)*
　　la-LA-la-la
　　la-LA-la…

(They dance off. Mymra fox-trots by with Mr. Robber.)

MYMRA: You know, I'm just crazy about pince-nez. I'll bet you're a passionate guy.

MR. ROBBER: Well…thanks.

(They dance off. The Stiff floats in from the salon, hoarsely singing the old song, "Styenka Razin," and conducting an invisible chorus.)

THE STIFF: *(Singing.)*
　　"From the island, down the river,
　　　On the current borne along…"
　　Slow down, basses!
　　　"Come canoes of every color—…"
　　Tenors, a little softer!
　　　"This is Styenka Razin's song!"

(Cherubim comes out of his alcove.)

Ah, *madame!* May I have this dance?

CHERUBIM: I no madama!

THE STIFF: You're not! Well, damn it to hell! They promised me madamas!

(Cherubim returns to his place. The Stiff sings.)

　　"And he flings her to the fishes,
　　　Casts her down beneath the waves!"

(He approaches a mannequin.)

Ah-ha! Here's a madama—and it's about time! Shall we have a little spin around the floor?…Whassamatter, not in the mood? Fine…You're smiling?…Smile, go ahead…smile today, you'll be crying tomorrow! Maybe you think I'm a stiff. You're making a big mistake. *(He approaches a second mannequin.)* Madame? *(The fox-trot music gets louder. He puts his arm around the mannequin and begins to dance.)* In all my life, I've never seen such a tiny waist. *(He gazes into the mannequin's eyes.)* Get away, you big phony! *(He throws the mannequin on the couch.)* I hope I never lay eyes on you again!

AMETISTOV: *(Appearing suddenly.)* Pardon, pardon. What is it, my most respected Ivan Vassilyevich? What can I do to make you happy?

THE STIFF: Just you wait! When my men get here, I'll string up the lot of you! *(He sings, dolefully.)*
"As our ship comes home to harbor,
We will toss the Communists…"

AMETISTOV: Oh now, Ivan Vassilyevich! Be nice! Let me bring you a little ammonia to clear your head.

THE STIFF: How dare you! Everyone else gets champagne, I get ammonia.

AMETISTOV: Ivan Vassilyevich, my dear…

(The door to Zoya's half-lit bedroom opens. Aliluya sneaks in, hides behind the drapes, and observes the proceedings. Mr. Robber and Mymra come in from the salon.)

MR. ROBBER: My God, Ivan Vassilyevich, are you soused! You should be ashamed of yourself! Where do you think you are, the "New Bavaria?"

THE STIFF: They're serving me ammonia!

MYMRA: My dear, my darling Ivan Vassilyevich, what's wrong with you?

AMETISTOV: Come with me to the dining room, Ivan Vassilyevich. You've got to eat something!

MYMRA: You naughty man! I'm yours tonight, although you don't deserve it.

THE STIFF: Get away from me, you traitor!

MYMRA: You awful man! Don't you remember me? I sat next to you at supper.

THE STIFF: So what? You sat next to me? *(He points to Ametistov.)* So did she! And what good did it do me?

MR. ROBBER: You have disgraced me forever, Ivan Vassilyevich. Marya Nikiforovna, my deepest apologies. Let me beg your forgiveness! *(He kneels.)*

MYMRA: Please, no, it's all right!

MR. ROBBER: *(On his knees.)* Forgive him. He's got a heart of gold. He's from Rostov-on-the-Don, he's just visiting. Everybody loves him. But you see...

THE STIFF: Go ahead, humiliate yourself. You worm!

AMETISTOV: Take his arm, Marya Nikiforovna. Come along, Ivan Vassilyevich.

THE STIFF: Thank you. You're the only one I can trust...Wait a minute, you rascal, don't I know you? You're from Voronezh!

(Ametistov and Mymra lead him off.)

ZOYA: *(Appearing, again as if by magic.)* Is everything all right?

MR. ROBBER: Zoya Denisovna, both for myself and in the name of Ivan Vassilyevich, I wish to offer you my deepest apologies. He can't help it, he's anemic, he's from Rostov-on-the-Don, and the champagne went to his head. On my knees, I beg you...

ZOYA: Oh, please, it's nothing. Although I really can't let him go home yet, not before...well, he seems to have forgotten...

MR. ROBBER: But of course, Zoya Denisovna, allow me...First, how much do I owe you?

ZOYA: Two hundred and ten rubles.

MR. ROBBER: Fine. And Ivan Vassilyevich?

ZOYA: The same. We all share equally.

MR. ROBBER: *(Counting out the money.)* Well, let's see...That's four hundred and, uh...

ZOYA: Twenty.

MR. ROBBER: Precisely. You're a mathematician! *Merci, merci.* Here you are...for both of us. What a marvelous party!

(From the salon, a fox-trot blares.)

Oh, Zoya Denisovna, will you honor me with a dance?

ZOYA: Sorry, I don't dance.

MR. ROBBER: No? What a shame!

(Mr. Robber goes back to the salon, closing the door behind him. Cherubim pops out of the alcove and looks toward the hallway, just in time to see Manyushka peeping in. She signals to Zoya. Zoya nods, and Alla Vadimovna, in a cloak and a hat with a veil, slips into the room.)

ZOYA: *(Quietly.)* Hello, Allachka. Show her where to go, Manyushka, and help her with her gown.

(Manyushka leads Alla off through Zoya's bedroom. Cherubim disappears. Aliluya steps out from behind the drapes, startling Zoya.)

Aliluya! What are you doing here? How did you get in?

ALILUYA: *(In a whisper.)* I came up the back way. I have keys to all the apartments, you know that. Well, well, well, Zoya Denisovna, shame, shame, shame! What a workshop! Now I get it.

ZOYA: Here. *(She gives him some money.)* Go away and keep your mouth shut. Come back after the party and I'll give you more.

ALILUYA: Please be careful, Zoya Denisovna!...

ZOYA: Go, go...

(Aliluya goes out through the bedroom. Zoya follows him. The door from the salon opens, and we hear people around the piano singing "The Moon Is Shining" as Abolyaninov plays. Goos enters. He closes the door behind him. He is unhappy.)

GOOS: Goos, you're drunk!...You're so drunk...the Coordinating Director of the Essential Metals Industries is so drunk...that there are no words to describe it!...And why is he so drunk?... He'll never tell, because he's too proud! Because Gooses are proud!...Beautiful women are swirling around him like mermaids and the whole staff is trying its best to entertain the Coordinating Director, but it's no good...His soul is dark with gloom. Oh, mannequin!...

(Zoya returns and listens, unobserved.)

...silent mannequin, of the French school, to you alone will I entrust my secret. I am...

ZOYA: In love!

GOOS: Oh, Zoyka! What a workshop! Never mind, it's all right. You're a genius! Would you like a certificate? "To whom it may concern: the bearer of this certificate is an Official Genius." I'll have them send you one...You heard everything I said, didn't you? Oh, well, what difference does it make? I've got a viper in my bosom, Zoya...Oh, Zoya, she's no good, I know it, but what can I do?

ZOYA: Why let her torment you, Goos? You'll find someone else.

GOOS: Show me someone else, Zoya. Someone who can make me forget her for a little while and tear her out of my heart...If you don't, there will be a tragedy in Moscow: Goos will ruin his life. Goos will break up his happy little family on Sadovaya Street and lose his two little ones, and a wife he respects...his two little ones who look as much like their papa as if we were all banknotes.

ZOYA: Oh, my poor Goos, my old friend, be patient! Before the night is over, I'll show you a woman who will make you forget everything. And she'll be yours, Goos, for how could she resist you?

ACT III

GOOS: You're so kind, Zoyka. Thank you.

(Ametistov comes in from the salon. Abolyaninov follows.)

Let me do something in return. How much does all this come to?

ZOYA: We divide the cost of our evenings among our guests, but you're my friend. I won't take anything from you!

GOOS: But I insist. When my heart is full, it's as big as the Volga. Here, five hundred rubles.

ZOYA: *Merci.*

GOOS: Get everyone in here, call them in.

ZOYA: Lizanka! Madame Ivanova!

GOOS: *(Making the sound of a cavalry charge.)* I have a little something for everyone!

AMETISTOV: The laborer is worthy of his hire. *Pardon, pardon.*

GOOS: Ah, the manager! The man who brought Paris to Sadovaya Street, and helped a suffering soul find consolation!

AMETISTOV: *Spécialité de la maison.*

GOOS: Here! *(He gives him money.)*

AMETISTOV: *Danke sehr.*

(Lizanka and Madame Ivanova come in from the salon.)

GOOS: Ah, the temple virgins, keepers of the flame!

LIZANKA: We aim to please, your excellency.

GOOS: Here!

(Goos kisses Madame Ivanova and gives her money.)

MADAME IVANOVA: You wild thing, you're like a Tartar chieftain…

GOOS: Here!

(Goos gives money to Lizanka.)

LIZANKA: *Merci.*

(Cherubim enters.)

GOOS: Ah, my Chinaman! Here you are, my cherub.

(He gives Cherubim money.)

Who's next? Have I missed anybody?

(Manyushka comes in.)

ZOYA: Stop, Boris Semyonich, that's enough! in times like these, in Soviet times, it makes no sense to be so generous.

GOOS: Don't worry, Zoya. Goos is a fountain that never runs dry. *(To Manyushka.)* The moon is shining, you say? Shine on, little Manyushka, shine away.

(He gives Manyushka money.)

MANYUSHKA: *Merci.*

THE POET: *(Leaping out with a yell.)* Lizanka, where are you?

GOOS: Here!

ACT III

(Goos offers him money.)

THE POET: But why, my esteemed Boris Semyonich?

GOOS: Don't argue with me.

THE POET: Well, in that case, permit me to present you with a little book of my poems…

GOOS: No, no! Permission denied! Leave it with my secretary.

(Ametistov brings Abolyaninov forward.)

AMETISTOV: Monsieur Abolyaninov!

GOOS: Count! What a piano player! Here!

(He gives Abolyaninov money.)

ABOLYANINOV: *Merci.* When things change, I'll have my seconds call on you.

GOOS: Fine! There's plenty for everybody! *(To a mannequin.)* Here!…

AMETISTOV: *(Guiding him away.)* Maestro, a march, please, in honor of Boris Semyonovich!

(Abolyaninov sits at the on-stage piano and plays a march.)

Pardon, pardon. This way, ladies and gentlemen! This way please! Find yourself a seat.

(From the salon come Mymra, The Foxtrotter, and Mr. Robber, arm-in-arm with The Stiff. Ametistov opens the alcove curtain.)

You too, please.

(The Smoker comes out and takes a seat.)

MR. ROBBER: You're a fairy godmother, Zoya Denisovna. What an enchanting evening!

THE STIFF: Enchanting? Sure! I ordered champagne, they gave me ammonia. In Rostov, you'd get your mug smashed in for that.

MR. ROBBER: What an awful thing to say! My apologies, Zoya Denisovna.

ZOYA: Over here, Boris Semyonovich…come sit with me.

(Goos crosses and sits with Zoya.)

AMETISTOV: *(In front of the curtain.) Mesdames et messieurs!* Tonight, as a very special treat, we take great pleasure in presenting the lilac gown! First shown at a reception for the President of France! Yours for a mere six thousand francs! *Atelier!*

(Cherubim draws the curtain. The atelier platform is filled with lilacs.)

Maestro, please!

(Abolyaninov plays a passionate waltz. Wearing the lilac gown, Alla moves out on the platform and promenades to the music.)

GOOS: What?…No, it can't be!…Oh, this is terrific!…

THE POET: Terrific!

ALL: Bravo! Wonderful! Bravo!

ALLA: Oh!

GOOS: "Oh!" How do you like that "oh?" Isn't this marvelous? It's Alla Vadimovna!

(General applause.)

ALLA: What are you doing here?

GOOS: Isn't that amazing? She asks me what I'm doing here, when that's exactly what I should be asking her!

ALLA: I'm working…I'm a model.

GOOS: A model! The woman I love! The woman that I, Goos, am planning to marry when I abandon my wife and my little ones, my two precious angels! She's a model! Don't you realize, unhappy woman, exactly where you are?

ALLA: Of course I do—in an *atelier.*

GOOS: *Atelier?!* It may be spelled *"atelier"* but it's pronounced "bordello!"

ALL: What? What did he say? What's going on?…

GOOS: Have you ever seen an *atelier,* dear comrades, where gowns are modeled after dark, while a "maestro" plays?

THE STIFF: You said it!…The hell with the music! Bring on the girls…

AMETISTOV: *Pardon, pardon.*

ZOYA: Ah-ha! Now I understand. *(She mimics Alla.)* "Since the death of my husband, Zoya Denisovna, there has been no one." Oh, you little phony! You liar! I even asked you, didn't I? I tried to warn you! Thanks a lot, Allachka!

THE POET: What's going on here?

MR. ROBBER: Isn't it obvious? *(He laughs.)*

GOOS: Zoya Denisovna, you have just introduced me to a "model" who happens to be my fiancée! *Merci!*

THE STIFF: Now, this is more like it!

ALLA: I'm not your fiancée!

GOOS: *(To Zoya.)* Just between you and me—she's my mistress!

THE STIFF: Oo-rah!

AMETISTOV: *Pardon, pardon!* Ivan Vassilyevich!

MR. ROBBER: What a scandal!

GOOS: Get this riffraff out of here, Zoya.

THE FOXTROTTER: I beg your pardon?

MYMRA: *(Swooning.)* Ohhh!

MR. ROBBER: You've gone too far, Boris Semyonich!

GOOS: Out! Everybody out!

ABOLYANINOV: *(Breaking off the waltz and looking around.)* What's going on?

ZOYA: I'm so sorry, my friends, for this little misunderstanding. I'm sure it can all be cleared up in a moment! Please, step into the salon. Sashka, take charge! Take charge!

AMETISTOV: *Pardon, pardon.* Please, everyone, come with me... They'll have a little private chat, and we'll have a big public fox-trot...We're not children, we know such things occasionally occur in polite society. Come, Ivan Vassilyich! Help me, Lizanka!

(Ametistov and Lizanka lead The Stiff into the salon.)

ZOYA: Pavlik, play a fox-trot! Immediately.

(Abolyaninov goes off.)

Madame Ivanova...

MADAME IVANOVA: *(To The Foxtrotter.)* Come on.

(Madame Ivanova throws her arms around The Foxtrotter, and she and the other women lead the men off to the salon, except for Cherubim and The Smoker, who return to the alcove. Zoya goes into her bedroom and closes the door. Shortly, however, she opens it a crack and stands listening. From the salon, the music of the fox-trot and the sounds of the party can be heard. Goos and Alla are alone. Then Ametistov reappears and slips behind the curtain, from which we can see him peeking.)

GOOS: You? In an *atelier?*...

ALLA: What are you doing here?

GOOS: What am I doing here? I'm a man! I wear pants, after all, not a dress slit up to the neck. I'm here because you have sucked the last drop of my blood. But why are you here?

ALLA: I'm here for the money!

GOOS: Oh, that's wonderful! And why do you need money?

ALLA: So I can go abroad.

GOOS: I won't give you money for that.

ALLA: That's why I'm here.

GOOS: Abroad!...Why not?...I'll bet all Paris is holding its breath. "Where's Alla Vadimovna?" The President of France is probably beside himself because Alla Vadimovna is not yet on her way.

ALLA: Yes, I'm sure he's beside himself...but not the President. My fiancé.

AMETISTOV: *(Peeking out from behind the curtain.)* Oh, ho!

GOOS: What? What did you say? If you have a fiancé in Paris, you're nothing but a tramp!

ALLA: I'm not! And don't you dare insult me!...I know it was wrong to deceive you, but I never thought you'd fall in love with me! I just wanted your money so that I could get away.

GOOS: Take my money, then, but stay!

ALLA: No, keep it, keep it! I can't take your money if you love me. I'll get what I need some other way, and then I'll go.

GOOS: I see! You've still got my rings on your fingers, but you'll get what you need some other way.

ALLA: Take them, then! I don't want them!

(She tears the rings off her fingers and throws them at Goos's feet.)

GOOS: I don't give a damn about the rings! Just answer me one thing—how long have you been coming here?

ALLA: This is my first time!

GOOS: You're lying, you viper.

ALLA: No, I'm not! I'm sick of lying!

GOOS: All right...Just answer me one thing—are you coming with me or not?

ALLA: I'm not!

GOOS: You're not? All right, I'll count to three. One!...Two!...Well, answer me!...I'll count to ten!

ALLA: You can count all you want, Boris Semyonich, but I'm not coming! I don't love you.

GOOS: You...whore!

(In the salon, the music breaks off abruptly, though the sounds of the party continue. Alla spits in Goos's face.)

(In a frenzy.) I must ask you not to spit!

AMETISTOV: *(Stepping forward.)* Or smoke, or mill about exchanging currency, or board the train from the center platform! *Pardon, pardon.* Boris Semyonich...

GOOS: Excuse me, I must ask you to leave!

AMETISTOV: *Pardon, pardon.*

GOOS: I said, excuse me...

AMETISTOV: And I said, *pardon, pardon...*

ABOLYANINOV: *(Appearing in the salon doorway.)* I must ask you not to insult a lady.

GOOS: Go away, piano-player.

ABOLYANINOV: Excuse me, but I'm not a piano-player.

ZOYA: *(Entering like a fury.)* Pavlik, what are you doing? Go play your piano!

(Abolyaninov goes out. To Alla.)

Well, thank you! Thank you very much! You elegant slut!

ALLA: Please don't insult me, Zoya Denisovna. I never dreamed that Boris Semyonich would visit your workshop. Good-bye. I'll send back your gown.

ZOYA: No, please, keep it...as a reward for your stupidity. You little fool!

(Alla starts to leave.)

GOOS: Stop! Where are you going? Paris?

ALLA: Yes, Paris. I'll escape if it kills me!

GOOS: Is that so? Here's what you'll get instead of a visa...*(He makes the sign of the fig.)*...or I'm not the man I think I am.

ALLA: I'll go without a visa!

GOOS: You'll never make it!

THE STIFF: *(In the salon doorway.)* Hey! No fair! We're missing all the fun! Down with the Chinese and the Latvians!

MR. ROBBER: *(Appearing behind him.)* Ivan Vassilyevich!

(He drags The Stiff back and closes the door.)

GOOS: You'll see! You'll end up selling everything you own at the Smolensk market. Piece by piece. I can just see you there, in your fancy lilac gown...or flat on your back in some hospital ward!

AMETISTOV: Alla Vadimovna, be so good as to...Manyushka!

(Manyushka appears in the hallway.)

Show her out.

(Alla leaves.)

GOOS: Alla, I love you! Alla, come back! I'll get you a visa! A visa!...Ohhh! *(He falls flat on the rug.)*

ZOYA: *(To Ametistov.)* Take care of him. *(She goes into the salon. As she opens the door, the fox-trot surges. She closes it behind her.)*

AMETISTOV: Oh, Boris Semyonich, the rug is dirty! Everything will be all right, you'll see...She's not the only girl in the world. Forget about her! *Entre nous soit dit*, she's not even pretty, she's *ordinaire*...

GOOS: Leave me alone! I'm grieving...

AMETISTOV: That's fine, you grieve a while...Here's cognac, and let's see...there are cigarettes on the table. Go ahead, grieve, grieve. *(He goes into the salon. Fox-trot.)*

GOOS: *(Grieving.)* Goos is grieving...Oh, how he's grieving! And why is poor Goos grieving? Because he's just been through a catastrophe...the tragedy of his life...His heart is broken! And just when everything was going so well. I've risen as high as a man can rise...even higher!...but love, treacherous love, has knocked me down, and here I am, lying on this rug like a carcass in the desert...And where is this rug?...On the floor of a bordello! Me, a Coordinating Director! Alla! Come back!

AMETISTOV: *(Popping in from the salon.)* Shhh, Boris Semyonich, not so loud! We don't want to awaken the masses, do we?...*(He disappears, closing the door.)*

GOOS: Alla! Come back!

(Cherubim appears and approaches silently.)

Leave me alone! I'm grieving...

CHERUBIM: Why so sad? You big man—sure, sure. Why so sad? *(He sees one of Alla's rings on the floor, scoops it up, and puts it in his pocket.)*

GOOS: Oh, my beautiful Chinese friend, my cherub...I can't bear to look at any other face but yours. Your innocent, angelic face...I'm racked with grief, that's why I'm down here on the rug...

CHERUBIM: Grief? Me, too!

GOOS: Oh, my Chinaman! Why are you grieving? You have your whole life ahead of you. You can still join the Party!...Alla! Alla!

CHERUBIM: Oh, grief for madama? All madama no good—sure, sure...So what? Get new madama!...Moscow plenty madama.

GOOS: But I can't get a new madama!

CHERUBIM: No money?

GOOS: Oh, my dear, innocent Chinaman! What an idea! Goos with no money? Maroon me on a desert island with my pockets empty, and the next day I'll be rolling in money. But what difference does it make? All the money in the world can't buy her love! Look! *(Out of his pockets he pulls fat rolls of banknotes.)*

CHERUBIM: So much money!

GOOS: This morning, I got five thousand rubles, and this evening— a blow that knocked me down! Look at me! Here lies Goos by the side of the road! Let every passerby spit on him as he spits on his money! *(He spits.)*

CHERUBIM: Spit on money? How can spit? You have money, no madama!...I have madama, no money! Let poor Chinaman touch money?...

GOOS: Touch it, touch it...

CHERUBIM: *(Caressing the money.)* Ah, money, money! Beautiful money...

GOOS: Can I ever forget her? Oh, let me forget! Alla...

(Cherubim whips out his Finnish knife and stabs Goos under the shoulder blade. Goos dies without a murmur.)

CHERUBIM: Money...money and warm Shanghai!!

(Cherubim quickly gathers up the money and puts it in his pocket, tears off Goos's watch and chain and the rings from his fingers, wipes his blade on Goos's jacket, hoists him into an armchair, puts an opium pipe in his hand, and turns down the lights.)

(In a whisper.) Manooska!

MANYUSHKA: *(Popping out.)* What?

CHERUBIM: Tssss, quiet! Now go Shanghai...take train...

MANYUSHKA: What have you done, you devil?

CHERUBIM: Goos…cut him, kill him…

MANYUSHKA: Oh…you devil!

CHERUBIM: You come now, or I cut you!

MANYUSHKA: Oh, God! Oh, my God!

(Manyushka runs off with Cherubim.)

AMETISTOV: *(Entering quietly.)* Boris Semyonich? *Pardon, pardon.* Are you resting? Go ahead, rest, relax! But where's Cherubim? He should be looking after you. It's easy to smoke too much when you're not used to it…and see, your hand is cold… *(He looks more closely.)* Wait a minute!…He's…He's been…murdered! Son-of-a-bitch! Well, comrades, this was certainly not on the agenda! Now what?…Ruined! Annihilated! Cherubim! Yes, of course!…robbed him and ran…What a bandit! And what a fool I've been!…Well, there goes Nice! There goes our only way out!

(Pause. Then, lethargically.)

"The stars are shimmering with light…" What am I doing? Why am I standing here? Run! *(He tears off his coat and tie, runs into Zoya's bedroom, opens a drawer, takes out some papers and banknotes and puts them in his pocket, gets his old suitcase from under the bed, takes out his old jacket and cap and puts them on.)* My faithful companion, my dear old bag, we're on our own again. But where are we going? Tell me, dear comrade, where shall we go? Oh, my star, my restless and wandering star!…Oh, my destiny!…Busted again!…Good-bye, Zoyechka. Forgive me! But what else can I do? Farewell, Zoyka's apartment! *(He leaves with his suitcase.)*

ZOYA: *(Entering.)* Aleksander Tarasovich! Oh, Boris Semyonovich, is that you? Are you alone?...You're not angry with me, are you? You know, that Alla Vadimovna is a complete mystery to me... *(She takes a closer look.)* Oh, my God! My God! We're lost! Oh, my God! *(She goes to the door, opens it, and calls quietly.)* Pavel Fyodorovich! Come here, please. *(The music stops.)* I'll send him right back, my friends...

ABOLYANINOV: *(Entering.)* What is it, Zoyechka?

ZOYA: Pavlik, it's a catastrophe! Look...Goos is dead! Murdered by the Chinaman—and Ametistov! We have to get out of here!

ABOLYANINOV: What are you talking about?

ZOYA: Wake up, Pavlik! There's a body in the armchair, and it's drenched in blood. We're finished.

ABOLYANINOV: Pardon me, Zoya, this is horrible, but how can anyone possibly blame us? Whatever those scoundrels may have done...and after all, we're not the ones who ran away!...

ZOYA: There's not a moment to lose, Pavlusha! We need our papers, our money...

(She runs to the bedroom. Abolyaninov rushes after her. A pause. From the hallway come Comrade Pestrukhin, Vanyichka, and Tubby, all wearing tuxedos and overcoats, followed by Gan-Tsa-Lin.)

COMRADE PESTRUKHIN: Deedle deedle dum, deedle dum.

GAN-TSA-LIN: Get Cherubimka first! He have knife!

TUBBY: All right now, take it easy.

COMRADE PESTRUKHIN: *(Seeing Goos.)* What's wrong with him? Too much opium?

VANYICHKA: A specialty of the house!

ZOYA: *(Off.)* Gone! All gone!

COMRADE PESTRUKHIN: Quiet.

(They hide. Zoya runs back in. Abolyaninov follows.)

ZOYA: Sashka took it, of course! So he's a thief, as well as a murderer. Let's go!

ABOLYANINOV: I can't fathom any of this, Zoya.

ZOYA: We don't have time to fathom!

ABOLYANINOV: And what about our guests?

ZOYA: Oh, Pavlushka, the hell with them! Run! *(She runs toward the hallway.)*

COMRADE PESTRUKHIN: *(Stepping out.)* Hold on there, citizen, what's your hurry?

ZOYA: Oh!

COMRADE PESTRUKHIN: Madam Peltz?

VANYICHKA: That's her all right.

ZOYA: What's going on? Who are you?

VANYICHKA: Take it easy, lady, we've got a warrant.

ZOYA: Oh, I see! You're here to investigate the crime.

COMRADE PESTRUKHIN: Good guess, Madam Peltz.

VANYICHKA: Isn't that the truth?

ZOYA: All right, here are the facts. Abolyaninov and I had nothing to do with it. It was the Chinaman—I don't even know his name—and that wretch Ametistov, whom I pitied and allowed into my apartment. They killed him and ran.

GAN-TSA-LIN: Cherubimka gone!!

COMRADE PESTRUKHIN: Killed him! Killed who?

ZOYA: Goos.

(Comrade Pestrukhin, Vanyichka, and Tubby hurl themselves toward the body.)

COMRADE PESTRUKHIN: I told you, Vanyichka! You should have held on to that Cherubimka.

GAN-TSA-LIN: Oh, Vanyichka! Let Cherubimka go?!

TUBBY: Shh, shh, shh, shh! Take it easy!

(Sounds of the party erupt in the salon.)

COMRADE PESTRUKHIN: Who's in there?

ZOYA: We're having a little party. It's my name-day.

COMRADE PESTRUKHIN: Uh-huh.

ZOYA: My guests had nothing to do with the murder!

COMRADE PESTRUKHIN: Vanyichka!

VANYICHKA: *(Opening the doors to the salon.)* All right, citizens, produce your papers!

TUBBY: *(On the telephone.)* Hello? 6-1-5-double 0. Comrade Kalancheyev? It's me…Oh, come on, me!…Listen, send over one of your boys and a coroner. Right. Number 10 Sadovaya Street, Apartment 504. And wire every railroad station: pick up Ametistov and Tsen-Tsin-Poh, alias "Cherubim."

(The party guests pour through the doors.)

MR. ROBBER: Pardon me, but there's been a big mistake…I'm not even supposed to be here…

THE POET: Oh, my God! Oh, my God!

LIZANKA: *(To Mymra.)* They've got us cornered.

MADAME IVANOVA: Some party!

COMRADE PESTRUKHIN: Papers, please! Your papers, citizens!

(General commotion. The Foxtrotter tries to sneak away.)

TUBBY: Hold it, you! Not so fast!

THE FOXTROTTER: I'm just here for the dancing…

MR. ROBBER: Pardon me, what seems to be the trouble? A little family name-day party—that's not against the law, is it? I'm a lawyer myself, you know.

TUBBY: There's been a murder in this apartment, Citizen Lawyer.

ALL: What? What did he say? No! Is it possible?

MYMRA: It's Goos! They killed Goos! *(She swoons.)*

MR. ROBBER: No! Monstrous!

ACT III

THE POET: Oh, Lord! *(He crosses himself.)*

(More commotion.)

MADAME IVANOVA: Now what?

LIZANKA: We'll pay forever for this crime, and once again, and one more time!

THE STIFF: *(Floating in.)* Well, finally. Reinforcements at last! Thank God! And not a minute too soon—I'm nearly dead of boredom! Hello, boys! Take off your coats, and stay a while. Let the good times begin! *(He starts to float out again.)*

MR. ROBBER: Shut up, you fool. There's been a murder here.

(More commotion.)

COMRADE PESTRUKHIN: Vanyichka, see if there's anybody else...

VANYICHKA: *(In the doorway.)* It's all clear, Comrade Pestrukhin.

GAN-TSA-LIN: Cherubimka gone!! Oh, Vanyichka!

ZOYA: Well now, my heroes in tuxedos, what's next? Who are you taking with you?

THE STIFF: Hey, where do you think you're going, comrades? Take off your coats!

ZOYA: Meanwhile, the real killers are getting away, running as fast as they can!

TUBBY: What are you talking about, lady? Where can they run? In the Soviet Union, running is not permitted. Everyone stays put.

VANYICHKA: Isn't that the truth?

(The doorbell rings.)

COMRADE PESTRUKHIN: Keep it down, citizens. Let Vanyichka open the door. Act as if nothing has happened.

(The doorbell rings again.)

THE STIFF: Right! Everybody shut up! Waiter! More champagne!

(Vanyichka lets in Aliluya.)

ALILUYA: Hello, citizens. Ah, Zoya Denisovna! Your party is still going on? The neighbors are complaining…

TUBBY: And who might you be, citizen?

ALILUYA: That's a good one. As a matter of fact, I'm the Chairman of the Apartment House Committee, so maybe I should be asking the questions.

TUBBY: Does the name Goos ring a bell?

ALILUYA: What's this all about? I'm here to see Zoya Denisovna. Let me through immediately.

COMRADE PESTRUKHIN: Answer the question, citizen.

ALILUYA: Who are you, anyway?…Uh, what was the question? Goos? Sure, of course I know him. Goos lives in our building, comrade.

TUBBY: Lived, citizen. Past tense.

ALILUYA: …As a matter of fact, dear comrades, I've had this little apartment under observation for a long time…On the surface, everything seemed to be all right, peaceful, quiet, but I had a funny feeling...I knew there was something fishy going on...As a matter of fact, I came up here tonight on a surveillance mission...

ZOYA: A surveillance mission?! You son-of-a-bitch!

ALILUYA: I was going to file my report first thing in the morning.

ZOYA: Listen to me, everyone! He's on the take! He's got a hundred-ruble note in his pocket right this minute, and I can tell you the serial number.

(Aliluya pulls out the banknote and stuffs it in his mouth.)

TUBBY: What's this? Are you demented? Gobbling up banknotes!

(Tubby forces Aliluya to spit out the banknote.)

ALILUYA: Forgive me, comrades, I'm a simple man. I'm still a little dazed, you know, from my service in the war years—all those hours bending over a lathe...You scared me, that's all.

TUBBY: Scared you? They're carving up Goos under your very nose and you're nibbling on banknotes, you swine of a chairman.

ALILUYA: My Lord Jesus Christ! *(He falls to his knees.)* Dear comrades, please take into consideration my humble beginnings in the ignorance and superstition that are the inescapable inheritance of the Tsarist times, and make your sentence conditional...what am I saying? I don't even understand it myself!

TUBBY: All right, all right. Get up.

ALILUYA: Comrade...

MR. ROBBER: May I use the telephone, please?

TUBBY: Telephoning is not permitted.

COMRADE PESTRUKHIN: Come along, citizens. And no talking on the way down. It will be better for you if you follow instructions.

MR. ROBBER: What do we have to talk about, anyway? The weather?

THE STIFF: "Ahoy and farewell," as the old parrot said. *(He sits down at the piano and plays a spirited march.)*

COMRADE PESTRUKHIN: *(To Tubby.)* Bring him. *(To The Stiff.)* That's a nice arrangement.

TUBBY: *(To Zoya.)* Put on your coat, citizen, it's time to go.

(Aliluya begins sobbing loudly.)

Stop bawling, you. Let's go.

ZOYA: My husband is not well. Please be gentle with him.

TUBBY: They'll put him in a hospital.

ZOYA: Farewell, my apartment. Farewell.

ABOLYANINOV: My head is spinning…tuxedos…blood…*(To Vanyichka.)* Excuse me, please, but why are you wearing tuxedos?

VANYICHKA: Well, we were coming to a party.

ABOLYANINOV: Ah…Forgive me, but with a tuxedo one never wears brown shoes.

VANYICHKA: *(To Tubby.)* You see? What did I tell you?!

END OF PLAY

PRONUNCIATION GUIDE

Mikhail Afanasyevich Bulgakov:
  mee-hah-EEL ah-fah-NAH-syeh-veetch bool-GAH-kuhf
Zoya Denisovna Peltz:
  ZOY-uh dyeh-NEE-suhv-nuh PELLTS
Zoyka:
  ZOY-kuh
Zoyechka:
  ZOY-eetch-kuh
Manyushka:
  muh-NYOO-shkuh
Manyusha:
  muh-NYOO-shuh
Marya Garbatova:
  MAHR-yuh gahr-BAH-tuh-vuh
Anisim Zotikovich Aliluya:
  ah-NEE-seem ZOH-tee-kuh-veetch ah-lee-LOO-yuh
Pavel Fyodorovich Abolyaninov:
  PAH-vyehl fee-OH-der-uh-veetch ah-buhl-YAH-nee-nuhf
Pavlik:
  PAHV-leek
Pavluha:
  pahv-LOOSH-uh
Pavlushka:
  pahv-LOOSH-kuh
Gan-Tsa-Lin:
  gahn-tsah-leen
Cherubim:
  CHAIR-oo-beem
Cherubimchik:
  chair-oo-BEEM-cheek
Cherubimka:
  chair-oo-BEEM-kuh
Tsen-Tsin-Poh:
  tsehn-tsihn-poh
Aleksander Tarasovich Ametistov:
  ah-leck-SAHN-der tah-RAH-suh-veetch ah-meh-TEES-tuhf
Varvara Nikanorovna:
  vahr-VAHR-uh nee-kuh-NOHR-uhv-nuh
Agnessa Ferapontovna:
  ahg-NYEHS-uh fyehr-uh-PONT-uhv-nuh
Varvara Nikolaevna:
  vahr-VAHR-uh nee-koh-LAH-yuhv-nuh
Alla Vadimovna:
  AH-luh vuh-DEEM-uhv-nuh

Allachka:
>AHL-utch-kuh

Mymra:
>MIHM-ruh

Marya Nikiforovna:
>MAHR-yuh nee-KEE-fuhr-uhv-nuh

Lizanka:
>LEE-zuhn-kuh

Madame Ivanova:
>ee-VAHN-uh-vuh

Boris Semyonovich Goos-Remontny:
>buh-REES seem-YOHN-uh-veetch GOOS ree-MONT-nih

Pestrukhin:
>pyeh-STROO-khihn

Vanyichka:
>VAHN-eetch-kuh

Vanya:
>VAHN-yuh

Robber:
>RAH-bur

Ivan Vassilyevich:
>ee-VAHN vuh-SEEL-yuh-veetch

Firsov:
>FEER-suhf

Sadovaya Street:
>sah-DOH-vah-yuh

Myura's:
>MYOO-ruhs

Svetnoy Boulevard:
>svyett-noy

Ostozhenka Street:
>oss-toh-ZHEN-kuh

Kursk:
>KOORSK

Vassily Ivanovich Putinkovsky:
>vuh-SEE-lee ee-VAHN-uh-veetch poo-teen-KOHF-skee

Baku:
>buh-KOO

GPU:
>GAY-pay-OO

Chernigov:
>chair-NEE-guhff

Rostov:
>ruh-STOHFF

Sevastopol:
>syeh-vuhs-TOH-puhl

PRONUNCIATION GUIDE

Stavropol:
  STAHV-ruh-puhl
Novocherkask:
  noh-voh-chair-KAHSK
Voronezh:
  vuh-ROHN-yehzh
Karl Petrovich Chemodanov:
  kahrl pyeh-TROH-veetch cheh-muh-DAHN-uhf
Anton Siguradze:
  ahn-TOHN see-goo-RAHD-zeh
Taganrog:
  tah-gahn-ROHG
Arbat Street:
  ahr-BAHT
Kuznetsky Bridge:
  kooz-NYETT-skee
Sepourakhina:
  syeh-poo-RAH-hee-nuh
papa, papachka:
  PAH-puh, PAH-puhtch-kuh
papasha:
  pah-PAH-shuh
Tretyakov Gallery:
  treh-tyuh-KOFF
Penza:
  PEHN-zuh
Tambov:
  tahm-BOHF
Lunacharsky:
  loo-nah-CHAR-skee
Lbov:
  11-BOHF
Kalancheyev:
  kah-lahn-CHAY-ehf
Samoteka Street:
  sah-muh-TYOH-kuh
Butyrski Castle:
  boo-TIHR-skee
Tverskaya Street:
  tvehr-SKIGH-uh
Soldatenkoffskaya Hospital:
  suhl-dah-tehn-KOHF-skigh-uh
Styenka Razin:
  STYEHN-kuh RAH-zihn

NOTE: Occasionally, in conversation, the patronymics may lose a syllable, informally—Aleksander Tarasovich becoming Aleksander Tarasich, Boris Semyonovich becoming Boris Semyonich, etc.

ZOYA: I had to bribe Aliluya today, so I only have 300 rubles left. That'll get us started. The apartment, that's all we have. And I'll squeeze everything I can out of it. We'll be in Paris by Christmas...We'll have a million francs, I guarantee it.

WHAT WILL BECOME OF US?:
The Importance of the Apartment

An Afterword for ZOYKA'S APARTMENT
by Frank Dwyer

• • •

ABOLYANINOV: (Off.) No, Zoya, not me, I'd be hopeless. The position requires an accomplished rascal.
AMETISTOV: (To himself.) Just in time!

1. PROLOGUE: MOSCOW, IN THE 20'S OF THE 20TH CENTURY.

We can perhaps determine the very moment that, for the Russians at least, the Twenties began to roar: on March 15, 1921, as Chief Commissar Vladimir Ilyich Lenin addressed the Tenth Congress of the Communist Party and proclaimed an astonishing philosophical and policy reversal. In order to revive an economy expiring from the calamitous effects of so-called "war communism," Lenin formally proposed a New Economic Policy, the NEP.

The first step was to resuscitate the farmers, so Lenin announced that the previous Soviet policy of requisitioning surpluses would be replaced by a regular, and more moderate, grain tax. (Before, as soon as the farmers realized there was no good reason to produce surpluses, surpluses had disappeared, and Russia was starving.)

The NEP would correct that, by permitting, after the new tax was paid, the free trade, sale and purchase of all surpluses, not only through cooperative organizations but also at "markets and bazaars." It also permitted the setting up of private enterprises, leased by the government. Profits could be produced. Capital could be accumulated. In the gray aftermath of war and revolution, it seemed something like a miracle; something, in fact, like freedom. The comrade-citizens shook off their Bolshevik stupor and began to compete, with unaccustomed (if not positively un-Russian) frenzy. Rubles began to flow.

A new class of entrepreneurs known as the Nepmen sprang up, seemingly overnight. Sensational accounts of their audacious embezzlements and tax-evasions soon filled the newspapers, and the general public viewed these fledgling tycoons with increasing suspicion; but with survival at stake in a world where the most basic rules had suddenly changed, it was almost impossible even for ordinary citizens to keep from being drawn into the NEP rat-race.

Bold, cunning, greedy, and unscrupulous, the Nepmen were shady mini-moguls dreaming the selfish dreams of the old American robber barons; and, like their 19th Century counterparts (Lenin must have been reading his Marx), they were necessary. Their combination of nerve, ambition, energy, and managerial skills made them the right men at the right time. The uninhibited enterprise of the Nepmen turned Moscow, in the early Twenties, into a kind of wild-West boom town. Anything went.

And however badly the Nepmen behaved, however precarious and uncertain their brave new world was, or temporary it might turn out to be, they were the outward and visible signs of a kind of liberation. Under the NEP, the individual could thrust his way up from the masses one last time, for better or worse, in a glorious swan song. Individual initiative would be rewarded, and there were heretofore unimaginable opportunities to display such initiative in the acquisition of rubles. If you were bold and cunning, like the Nepmen, and had a little bit of luck, anything was possible. The sky had cleared, and on a high enough pile of rubles, you could see the Eiffel Tower. The paradise of Paris was at hand: if your timing was right, you might be able to get away before Lenin changed his mind and the sky shut down again, as you knew it must.

Just as the Muscovites were beginning to make the difficult transition from the paralysis of the post-war Soviet economy to the pandemonium of the NEP, an elegant, ironic, keenly observant, brilliantly witty young writer, Mikhail Bulgakov, arrived from a great provincial capital, confidently expecting to make his name and fortune, or, at the very least, a living, in the new capital. Though still pining for a lost world, for the grace, culture, and serenity of his pre-Revolutionary childhood and youth in Kiev, Bulgakov quickly learned to scramble, as all Moscow was scrambling, to adapt himself to the new set of sometimes ambiguous rules. His survival depended on it. Bulgakov survived. Over the next two decades, in fact, he displayed an almost unique talent for surviving—only just—with his integrity intact and the fires of his creativity still burning.

Bulgakov did more than survive. He also managed to preserve for posterity the amazing, ridiculous reality, the ache of hope, the pulse of terror, the liberation of laughter, of that evanescent epoch, in ZOYKA'S APARTMENT, a comic masterpiece which he called, for very good reasons, a "tragic farce." Written in five days toward the end of 1925 and extensively revised a decade later, ZOYKA'S APARTMENT is the only one of Bulgakov's plays set in contemporary Moscow. In it, he captures the sense and essence of Moscow under the NEP, the panic and exhilaration, the sounds, the colors, the very atmosphere, of those heady, dangerous days. Before taking a closer look at the play, it may be useful to see who this playwright was and how he came to be able to write it.

• • •

AMETISTOV: We got lost in the memories of our childhood...We grew up together, you know, didn't we, Zoyechka? A moment ago, I was actually weeping...

2. KIEV: THE TENDER SNOW

Mikhail Afanasievich Bulgakov was born on May 15, 1891 (May 3 in the Old Style; Russia did not adopt the Gregorian calendar until 1918) into a big, happy Russian family in what he would later call "the most beautiful town in Russia," Kiev, the quiet, old-fashioned, essentially Russian capital of the backward, agricultural, un-Russian province of the Ukraine. He was the eldest of seven surviving children of Afanasy Ivanovich Bulgakov, Divinity Professor at Kiev Theological Academy, and his vivacious and intelligent young wife, Varvara Mikhailovna. Mikhail's mother was a blue-eyed blonde, and he was blond, too, with striking light blue eyes. His paternal grandfather was a small-town priest, his maternal grandfather a bishop, and the family tree blossomed with priests, government officials, teachers, and doctors.

The growing family, further enlarged by the addition of Afanasy Ivanovich's mother and several young cousins from the country, moved several times before coming to rest in 1907 at # 13 St. Andrew's Hill, on a picturesque street in a lovely neighborhood, where they rented eight rooms on the top floor of a handsome, sprawling 2-story building. (The house, now a historical landmark, is described in loving detail in Mikhail's first novel, THE WHITE GUARD; it's the home of the Turbins.)

It was a house full of music. Father played the violin, mother and Mikhail the piano, brother Ivan the balalaika—in fact, everyone played an instrument or sang in a choir. (Mikhail's mother is reported to have drawn the line only when one of her sons brought home a trombone.) Father liked cards, mother the theater, and they entertained frequently.

As was to be expected in this nest of gentlefolk, there was a great emphasis on education. Mikhail was an independent, fanciful boy, famous at school for fighting, for jokes and tricks, and for telling such compelling stories that his listeners were never sure whether they were made-up or true. He wrote his first story at 7. He read DEAD SOULS at 9 and ever after acknowledged Gogol as his master. (His godfather was a Gogol scholar who taught at his school.) "Wherever Misha was," a friend of the family wrote, "jokes, laughter, gaiety and wit reigned."

Mikhail soon learned to share his mother's passion for theater (Kiev's illustrious Solovtsov Theater offered a steady fare of Russian and French classics), and he was especially fond of the opera. For a time, he thought of becoming an opera singer, and he learned arias and duets. His sister Vera said that he saw his favorite opera, Gounod's FAUST, at least 41 times.

In 1900, Afanasy Ivanovich bought land in the village of Bucha. His boys helped him clear the grounds, make paths, and plant flower and vegetable gardens, and from 1902 the Bulgakovs spent merry summers at the dacha there. The children ran barefoot, and Mikhail organized amateur theatricals in which the whole family took part. He called his family repertory company the Pickwick Club, after the novel by Dickens.

In 1905, when Father Gyorgy Gapon led the march of peaceful petitioners toward the tsar's palace in St. Petersburg on what would come to be called Bloody Sunday, Mikhail was a 13-year-old schoolboy. The events of that fateful year, the rehearsal for the Russian Revolution, do not seem to have much disturbed the tranquility of sleepy Kiev or the big house at St. Andrew's Hill.

A more intimate calamity did touch the Bulgakovs the following year: Mikhail's father fell gravely ill with sclerosis of the kidneys. His loving colleagues at the Theological Academy managed to make him a Doctor of Theology (the larger pension would help provide for their friend's large family) just before he died, in 1907. He was 48.

Mikhail graduated from high school in 1909; and, despite his passion for literature and music, he decided to study medicine. His mother's brothers were doctors. So was Ivan Pavlovich Voskresensky, the old family friend and neighbor who would later become Mikhail's stepfather. For her part, Varvara Mikhailovna wanted all her sons to be engineers, but Mikhail saw medicine as a "brilliant" career and entered Kiev's St. Vladimir Imperial University in 1909. He still devoted so much time and energy to writing and amateur theatricals, however, that he was forced to repeat the second year.

He had another distraction, too. Around this time he met Tatyana (Tasya) Nikolayevna Lappa, the niece of one of his mother's best friends. Tasya was visiting Kiev from her home in Saratov, where her father was a government official. Misha was 18, Tasya 14; and though neither family encouraged the match, they were married four years later, in 1913. The young writer gently mocked the less-than-happy families in a little play he wrote to mark the occasion. (Tasya later revealed that Misha had gotten her pregnant and arranged an abortion for her before she graduated from high school.)

In 1923, Bulgakov wrote a long piece about "The City of Kiev." He longingly recalled those "legendary times," when

a lighthearted generation of young people never doubted that life would pass quietly, tranquilly—in white blossoms, dawns, sunsets, the Dnieper, the Kreshchatik, sunny streets in the summer, snow in the winter, but snow which would not be cold and cruel, large-flaked snow, tender and caressing.

Instead, he observed, "history intervened."

In 1916, he received his medical degree, with honors and was called up for military service. Russia had already been at war for two years.

By the time that we can articulate a perception of childhood, it has become, at least in part, a memory; and a happy childhood, even in a quiet life, is remembered with mingled joy and sorrow, a memory of loss, of an accumulation of losses. We grieve for the once-bright things forever laid by. We are creatures aware of time passing, aware that we ourselves are always moving on. The happy child, who has so much to be thankful for, often has surprisingly deep reserves of melancholy, too. He knows that his grief, however distant, lies onward, and some part of his joy behind.

The peculiar grace of Mikhail Bulgakov's writing, the energy, confidence, and merry heart that he reveals everywhere, from his most casual feuilletons to his great novel, THE MASTER AND MARGARITA, may well spring from what he called the "legendary times," the years of his youth in Kiev; but those times were also the source of that strain of Arcadian melancholy, of an intense if inchoate yearning for "another life...a distant shore," that also runs through his work. No one can bend back the hands of the clock and go home again, but the turbulent history of Bulgakov's time and place rendered even his happiest memories of home insubstantial, as if history had rudely awakened him from a beautiful dream. His works reveal a profound dislocation and sense of loss. They can be read as a continuing effort to reconcile irreconcilable realities of past and present, but also as a cumulative elegy for paradise lost, an elegy sometimes bewildered and subliminal (as in the quiet lamentations of Abolyaninov), and sometimes conscious and articulate (as in the long mourning of his novel, THE WHITE GUARD). The idiosyncratic equipoise of melancholy and a merry heart provides the distinctive texture and flavor of Bulgakov's work.

● ● ●

AMETISTOV: Oh, well, you know the rest...more Whites, more Reds, and there I go, bouncing around the whole Soviet System.

3. NIKOLSKOYE, VYAZMA CITY, KIEV: THE DAYS OF THE BULGAKOVS

As a doctor, Mikhail was spared active duty. Assigned to the reserves and awaiting his posting, he volunteered for the Red Cross, which sent him to several hospitals at the front.

In September, he was assigned to a zemstvo (local council) clinic in the distant village of Nikolskoye in Smolensk Province.

For the cosmpolitan young doctor, Nikolskoye seemed the end of the earth. He was on his own, learning on the job. Though he often had to look things up quickly in his medical books, he did well in Nikolskoye, managing difficult births, performing amputations, abortions, even a tracheotomy, with only Tasya to help him. He complained bitterly about the isolation and boredom of village life. In the course of his practice, he was amazed to find how widespread venereal diseases were, and how much suffering they caused the innocent, particularly children. He decided to specialize in venereology. Accidentally exposed to diphtheria, the young doctor took morphine to help him bear the painful anti-diphtheria treatment, and he developed an addiction to the drug.

To his great relief, he was transferred to the Vyazma City Zemstvo Hospital, near Moscow, in September, 1917. He and Tasya rejoiced at returning to civilization, but with other doctors around, he found it more difficult to prescribe himself morphine. He only managed to defeat the addiction when Tasya refused to take any more fake prescriptions to the different pharmacies.

He requested and was finally granted a discharge from the reserves in February 1918, and returned to the big house on St. Andrew's Hill. He stayed there until 1919, during what was perhaps the most troubled period in Kiev's history.

The tsar, Nicholas II, had abdicated in March 1917 and been replaced by a liberal Provisional Government, first under Prince Lvov and then under Aleksander Kerensky. Kerensky's government was overthrown by the Bolsheviks in November (October by the Russian Calendar: hence "the October Revolution"), and Lenin became Chief Commissar. In January 1918, in Kiev, a Ukrainian national assembly declared Ukraine an independent nation and, on February 9, negotiated a separate peace with the Central Powers at Brest-Litovsk.

Nine days later, the Bolsheviks (or "Reds") attacked and captured Kiev, but the Germans drove out the Bolsheviks on March 2 and restored the Ukrainian assembly. Then, in order to achieve greater control of vitally important Ukrainian grain, the Germans changed their minds and replaced the assembly with a puppet government, a hetmanate, under the former tsarist Gen. Pavel Skoropadsky.

The war ended on November 11, 1918, and soon the defeated Germans began to withdraw. The hetmanate quickly fell to a Ukrainian National Army under the bloody, vengeful Gen. Semyon Petlyura, whose six-week reign of terror ended on February 3, 1919, when he and his men fled from the approaching Reds. The Reds proclaimed the Ukraine a Soviet Republic, but were themselves driven out six months later by the White Guard (or "Whites"), a Volunteer Army under Gen. Anton Denikin.

Four months later, in December, the Reds decisively defeated the Whites. In May 1920, they repulsed a Polish invasion. On December 30, 1920, the Ukraine officially became part of the Union of Soviet Socialist Republics.

The great storm lashed the big house on St. Andrew's Hill. Bulgakov later calculated that there were 14 changes of power in Kiev, ten of which he himself experienced. (Ametistov's breezy account to Zoya of his adventures during this period gives us some sense of those dizzying, potentially-hazardous, and ultimately absurd changes.) His brother Nikolai and cousin Kostya went off in December 1918 to defend their city (and the hetmanate) against the approaching nationalists. Tasya said that Mikhail, too, went off at that time intending to fight but came back demoralized by the crushing defeat administered by Petlyura's troops. Nikolai and Kostya were missing. Mikhail searched diligently for them, even in the morgue: Petlyura's men regularly tortured and executed their opponents. Bulgakov, who had been mobilized by the hetmanate, was soon mobilized again, this time by the nationalists. (Doctors were always in demand. In Boris Pasternak's novel, Dr. Zhivago is also mobilized by the enemy.) Bulgakov managed to desert and run home, a very dangerous act, as the nationalists fled from the approaching Reds.

The family had no word from Nikolai and cousin Kostya until September, when they got a note from Kostya. He and Nikolai were in Pyatigorsk. Kostya was a captain with the Terek Cossacks and Nikolai, a cavalryman, was recovering from typhus. Bulgakov quickly got himself mobilized by the Whites and assigned to the Cossacks in Pyatigorsk, but his relatives had moved on by the time he got there, and both were wounded in fierce battles with the nationalists. Bulgakov finally caught up with Nikolai, but he couldn't talk him into going home.

While Bulgakov was searching for Nikolai, their youngest brother, Ivan, was called out of high school to help defend the city. After being wounded in the leg, Ivan deserted his post, and he and a friend attached themselves to the retreating Whites in order to get away from the continuous warfare. It was six months before word got back to St. Andrew's Hill that they were safe in Bavaria, living with friends and trying to finish high school.

Bulgakov was assigned to convoy seriously wounded soldiers who were being evacuated to Vladikavkaz, and he came to an important decision on that journey. This is how he later described it:

> One night, late in the fall of 1919, on a rolling train, by the light of a candle stuck in a kerosene bottle, I wrote my first little story. The train carried me away to a small town, where I took my story to the editors of the local newspaper. They published it. Then they published several feuilletons. At the beginning of 1920, I abandoned my degree with honors and became a writer.

• • •

ABOLYANINOV: I had a visitor today, a big lummox in tall boots, reeking of vodka. He came into my room and walked right up to me. "You're a former Count, aren't you?" he asked. "I beg your pardon," I said, "what does that mean exactly, `a former Count'? Did I vanish into thin air? Here I stand, as a matter of fact, before your very eyes...

4. VLADIKAVKAZ: A FORMER WRITER

Bulgakov may have been glad to go to Vladikavkaz because, deep in White territory, it seemed safer. When he got there, he obtained another transfer to the reserves and was given permission to work for a local newspaper, "The Caucasus"; but the paper failed, and Bulgakov fell ill with typhus When he recovered a month later, he learned that the Whites had retreated, and the Reds were now running the city.

Somehow he fell into an official job with the Reds: Literary Manager of the Arts Department of the People's Education Office. (Ametistov seems to have had a similar experience:

ZOYA: So...what have you been up to these past seven years?

AMETISTOV: Oh, cousin!...In 1919, I'm Director-in-Chief of the Chernigov Bureau of Art and Culture....)

At the Arts Department, Bulgakov tried to encourage local writers and to disseminate culture. In the political climate of the day, such seemingly innocuous ambitions were fraught with danger. Bulgakov proved to be a most controversial Literary Manager, sharply attacked by militant, decidedly unliterary local critics for championing such out-dated, bourgeois artists as Pushkin and Gogol. However he tried to adapt, Bulgakov's heart was clearly not in any great political adventure that would sweep away Pushkin and Gogol. Bulgakov was suspect, unsound: clearly a man from a different world, with a different sensibility; and proud of it! He made many enemies, who dismissed him as a "former" writer. (Abolyaninov is amazed by this epithet and mocks it several times, with amusing aristocratic disdain.)

Bulgakov fell sick again with typhus, and this time woke up to find that he and the rest of the unsound Arts Department had been fired. Eager to secure some other source of income, and perceiving what he thought was a great local need for new plays, he became a playwright. He dashed off four plays, but despite some success at Vladikavkaz's First Soviet Theater (where Tasya found employment, too, as an extra and a member of the corps de ballet), he despised these early works and later destroyed the manuscripts. (At least one has survived, in typescript.)

Bulgakov had a difficult time in the Caucasus. He spent most of his time and energy just trying to stay alive, but he was increasingly distressed by a consciousness of being behind schedule, of not yet having produced a collection of stories or made any kind of name for himself. How could he be a "former" writer when he was hardly a writer at all?

In desperate circumstances, he agreed to collaborate with a local lawyer on what he knew would be a dreadful play, then bragged about his ambiguous achievement, challenging the playwrights of Paris and Berlin to try and write anything worse. The play, THE SONS OF THE MULLAH, was nevertheless accepted by the new Vladikavkaz Arts Department and produced early in 1921 with great success.

With a little extra money, Bulgakov could get out of Vladikavkaz, perhaps even out of Russia. He went to Tiflis, the capital of Georgia, then Batum, the crowded Black Sea port that served as the principal embarkation point for emigrants on their way to Constantinople. In Batum, he sold his overcoat and tried to board ship for Constantinople, but was turned back. Running out of money, he fell sick again. When he recovered, he seems to have had no more thought, at that time, of emigrating. Instead, he sent Tasya to Moscow, to see if she thought they could manage to live there; and he returned disconsolately to Kiev. Later, from Moscow, he wrote his mother a letter describing that interlude at St. Andrew's Hill, lying on her couch and "drinking tea with French rolls," as the "happiest memory of recent times."

• • •

AMETISTOV: Aaaah, Moscow! Such wonderful beer! So, you managed to hold on to the apartment, Zoyka. Good for you!

5. MOSCOW: A CALLING WITHOUT DISTINCTION

Moscow was having a bad winter in 1921 and Bulgakov's journey was very difficult. When his money ran out, he had to walk the last hundred miles, following the railroad tracks. He arrived at night, towards the end of September. "I cannot describe how frozen I was," he later wrote. "I froze and ran. Ran and froze." He said he thought he saw a lottery ticket lying in front of him, marked with a single word: death. (There's a grim private irony in the lines he gives Ametistov, complaining bitterly about a much easier arrival:

Whew! Son-of-a-bitch! Dragging myself all the way from Kursk Station, up five long flights, lugging this old suitcase of mine! That's no small feat, believe you me...two whole miles, at least!...What I'd give for a bottle of beer!....)

By some miracle, Bulgakov quickly found a job as secretary of the Literary and Publishing Section under the People's Commissariat of Enlightenment, or LITO. Unfortunately, he wrote, LITO had no "chairs or tables, or ink or lamps, or books, or writers or readers."

Jobs were hard to find, but apartments were harder. He and Tasya moved in with his sister Nadya, and they fought to hold on to the communal apartment when Nadya and her husband returned to Kiev. They had a single room, and shared a kitchen and bathroom, on the top floor of a big and impressive apartment building at Number 10 Sadovaya Street called Pigit House. Five stories high, with spacious balconies and a large garden behind a wrought-iron fence, Pigit House loomed over its neighbors. It was a building with a history. The great stage director Vsevolod Meyerhold had lived there, Sergey Yesenin met Isadora Duncan there, and Fanny Kaplan hid there after her unsuccessful attempt to assassinate Lenin.

Bulgakov set ZOYKA'S APARTMENT in Pigit House, of course; he even gives us the actual address. By the time he got there, however, the character of the building had changed. Most of the intellectuals had decamped, and the Soviets had turned it into the first workers' commune. (That's the context for Aliluya's threat: "All right, that's it! If I don't allocate at least one room in this apartment to some deserving worker by sundown tomorrow, may I die like a dog!" Aliluya is the type of the officious building manager, who registers and spies on the other tenants to protect public and private morality. This new class of self-important busybodies, as Nadezhda Mandelstam reported in her powerful memoir, HOPE ABANDONED, "sprang up like mushrooms" after the Revolution.)

Bulgakov hated the "huge apartment building" and its "large, noisy courtyard," the lack of privacy, the "infernal music box of noise." "I waited for the night with all the impatience of a young man waiting for his beloved," says the protagonist of his autobiographical THEATRICAL NOVEL. "Only then was it quiet enough in my accursed room." (Abolyaninov, who seems to share Bulgakov's yearning for "another life...a distant shore" as well as his craving for morphine, has this to say about Pigit House and its ambiance:

This is such a terrible place, Zoya. My God, these people are so noisy! And the sunset, the sunset on Sadovaya Street is so disgusting. An obscene sunset. Shut the blinds! Shut them, shut them!)

Bulgakov was not finished with Pigit House after ZOYKA'S APARTMENT. It pops up again, in THE MASTER AND MARGARITA: where else in Moscow would the Devil himself take an apartment?

However he hated the apartment, Bulgakov could only cling to it fiercely as he hurled himself into the fray. He described his situation in a letter to his mother on November 17, 1921:

I can tell you, briefly, that what is happening here is a desperate struggle to survive by adapting to the new circumstances...Things will be particularly difficult at the end of November and in December, the very moment of transition to private enterprise. I'm relying on a multitude of friends and, frankly, on myself, on my own exertions....Moscow is changing, returning to a way of life not seen here for a long time—savage competition, rushing around in a frenzy, showing initiative, etc. There's no alternative now, if you want to survive.

His only dream, he wrote, was to live through the winter.

His LITO job soon ended; he and his colleagues were not surprised. They had seen the handwriting on the wall the day they were paid in matches. He found another job as the trade chronicle editor of a small business journal, but it soon folded, too.

Meanwhile, he was trying to do his own work, writing the stories about his time in Nikolskoye and Vyazma City, and his literary apprenticeship in the Caucasus, that would later be published as, respectively, NOTES OF A YOUNG DOCTOR and NOTES ON THE CUFF. (The typist who began transcribing NOTES ON THE CUFF that fall deferred her salary for years, sure that Bulgakov would pay her when he could, which he did.)

In the winter of 1922, Bulgakov's long-missing brother Nikolai finally got a message to the family. He and Ivan had escaped and were safely abroad. Nikolai was in Zagreb, in medical school. Bulgakov's mother died of typhus before receiving the good news.

In his diary, Bulgakov noted that he and Tasya were starving. In desperation, he joined a troop of strolling players, earning next to nothing. He also found some work as the master of ceremonies at a small theater.

Soon, he began writing regularly for an important emigré journal, "Nakanunye" ("On the Eve"), which had its central office in Berlin and a Moscow office in the colossal Nirenzee House, at ten stories the tallest building in the city. A group of Russian emigrés in Berlin had published a collection of articles called "Changing Landmarks," in which they argued that it was now time to accept the revolution as an accomplished fact. They applauded the NEP as a return to capitalism, urged all their fellow emigrés to be Russian patriots even if they could not accept the entire Marxist-Leninist line, and finally advocated return to the Soviet Union. "Nakanunye" was the organ of their movement.

In addition to a regular economics section and a book review, "Nakanunye" published a literary supplement, edited by Count Aleksei Tolstoy, one of the most prestigious of the emigrés. Tolstoy relished Bulgakov's wry sense of humor and demanded "more Bulgakov" from his Moscow office.

Bulgakov also began to work for another paper, "Gudok" ("The Whistle"), the organ of the railway workers' union, which had its offices, along with many other union organizations, in Moscow's House of Labor. His job at "Gudok" was to edit letters from the readers, making them either more coherent or funnier, and to provide feuilletons, the generally brief humorous or descriptive sketches which were the entertainment staples of Russian papers.

Bulgakov seems to have considered his "Nakanunye" pieces more significant, since he published them under his own name. (They were the source of his growing reputation.) He signed his "Gudok" feuilletons with a wide variety of amusing pseudonyms, including "M. Ol-rayt" (a literal transcription of the English phrase "I'm all right"); "G. P. Ukhov" (a dangerously irreverent appropriation of the initials of the Soviet secret police); and "Emma B." (a play on his own initials).

At the "Gudok" office, he fraternized with colleagues who would also come to be leading writers of the period, including his fellow Ukrainians Valentin Kataev, Yuri Olyesha, and Evgeny Petrov, Kataev's brother. (Petrov and his collaborator Ilya Ilf left a vivid satirical picture of those days in their novel TWELVE CHAIRS.) Bulgakov frequently dropped by other offices in the building to tell funny stories, which the other writers would turn into feuilletons of their own, and pick up a small fee for his contribution.

As a journalist, Bulgakov flourished, and he cut a dashing if eccentric figure as he raced around Moscow. Older than most of his colleagues, he seemed determined to set himself apart. Contemporaries describe him as elegant and meticulous, his clothes fine (if threadbare, and not of the latest fashion), his trousers always pressed, his collar unfailingly stiff and gleaming, his tie in a fancy knot, his hair neatly parted and lacquered with brilliantine, his face freshly shaved. (He shaved twice a day.) He affected a worn but distinguished fur coat and cultivated an old-fashioned way of speaking, of kissing ladies' hands, of practicing elaborate formal bows, as if he too wanted to belong, as Zoya says of her Pavlik, "in some Museum of the Revolution." Even in those more innocent days, when the Soviet Union was still young, such behavior was not without risk, which Bulgakov (like Abolyaninov) seemed slow to fathom. Later, responding to intensifying criticism of his work, criticism from a party line that found Pushkin and Gogol irrelevant in the workers' paradise, Bulgakov took to wearing a monocle. He apparently intended the sartorial provocation as a joke, but for a writer savagely attacked for looking backward with longing instead of forward with selfless dedication, it was a dangerous joke.

Though newspaper work now provided him a steady income, Bulgakov hated it. He said it only took him eighteen to twenty-two minutes to write a sketch of seventy or a hundred lines, and that included "time out for smoking and whistling." It took only eight minutes more to have the sketch transcribed, and that included time for "mild flirtation" with the typist. At the end of half an hour, then, he had finished his work for the day. He enjoyed hobnobbing with his colleagues on the "Nakanunye" staff, including the story writer Mikhail Zoshchenko and the poets Sergey Yesenin and Osip Mandelstam, as well as his old friends Kataev, Ilf, and Petrov, but he hated sitting around in the editor's office (he hated editors), waiting to be allowed to go home. That was time stolen away from his own work.

• • •

ABOLYANINOV: So many memories are coming back to me...

6. MOSCOW: *THE WHITE GUARD*

In spite of the time he wasted supporting himself with feuilletons, Bulgakov's own work was progressing. A censored first part of his NOTES ON THE CUFF appeared in "Nakanunye" in June 1922, and a second part in the prestigious literary journal "Rossiya." The "Rossiya" edition restored some of the "Nakanunye" cuts (references, for example, to his desire to leave the country, and descriptions of his controversial literary evenings) but also made new ones. (Only those parts of the manuscript published in one journal or the other seem to have survived.)

He was writing serious fiction, too, including stories that appeared in "Nakanunye" and stories and feuilletons that had appeared in "Gudok." (They were collected and published in two small volumes, A TREATISE ON HOUSING and STORIES, in 1926.) A long Gogolian story, "Diaboliad," was published in 1924, in an issue of "Nyedra," an anthology series. Another important story, "The Fatal Eggs," inspired by H. G. Wells's novel, THE FOOD OF THE GODS, was published in the February 1925 issue of "Nyedra." "The Fatal Eggs" was set slightly in the future and cunningly posed as science fiction in order to explore contemporary questions. The same month he completed one of his finest works, the satirical novella called THE HEART OF A DOG, which was rejected by "Nyedra" for political reasons.

Bulgakov's work was increasingly controversial, his satire, science fiction, humorous exaggeration, fantasy, etc. all clearly part of a continuing critique of the uncriticizable, the conditions of Soviet society. (THE HEART OF A DOG was not published during his lifetime. It appeared finally in German and English magazines in 1968, and as a book in Paris in 1969. The only substantial book he ever saw published in his homeland was DIABOLIAD, a collection of five stories including "Diaboliad" and "The Fatal Eggs," that appeared in May 1925.)

All this time, he was also working on a bigger project, his first novel, THE WHITE GUARD, which tells the story of the bloody battle for Kiev from the point-of-view of the Turbins, a close, loving Kiev family of the liberal intelligentsia, sympathetic to the "Whites" and very much like his own. ("Turbin," in fact, was his maternal grandmother's maiden name.) THE WHITE GUARD provides a fairly accurate account of events in Kiev in 1918-1919: the collapse of the hetmanate, the taking of the city by the brutal Ukrainian nationalists, Gen. Petlyura's 47-day reign-of-terror, and the flight of the nationalists at the approach of the triumphant Bolsheviks.

The book is more, however, than a record of bloodshed and savagery. It is also an elegy for the tender snow of Bulgakov's childhood, for a world and a way of life, now gone, that seem increasingly precious as the writer and his readers look longingly backward from the Soviet present. Bulgakov had been thinking about this book a long time, and may have started it a number of times, but he seems to have begun writing it in earnest only after the death of his mother, as if stung by a realization of how fragile the past is, and how fleeting even an excellent memory like his.

The first two parts of THE WHITE GUARD were published in "Rossiya" in 1924, but the journal was forced to suspend publication (partly because of THE WHITE GUARD) before it could print the final third. (The complete novel was not published in Russia in Bulgakov's lifetime, although he did correct the proofs for a Russian edition that appeared in Paris in 1929.)

A great change took place in his life in 1924. In January, the month Lenin died, Bulgakov went to a party celebrating the return of some of the "Changing Landmarks" emigrés, including the "Nakanunye" editor Count Tolstoy. He went without Tasya. His wife of 11 years was considerably less sophisticated than the women in his Moscow set, and she accompanied him less and less frequently.

At the "Changing Landmarks" party he met Lyubov Yevgenyevna Belozerskaya, the attractive, lively, sophisticated wife of one of the emigrés, the well-known satirical writer I. Vasilevsky (who published under the pseudonym "Nye-Bukva"). Lyubov admired Bulgakov's work and was eager to meet him. She liked him right away, but teased him about the color of his shoes. ("Chicken shoes" she called them; she hurt his feelings.) Unlike Tasya, Lyubov was an intellectual, a confident participant in the literary world; Tasya could not compete with her. A few months later, Lyubov ended her marriage, and Bulgakov divorced Tasya. Though Lyubov resisted him at first, Bulgakov persuaded her to become his wife, and they were married early that summer.

The newly-weds, broke and with no place to live, moved in with Bulgakov's generous sister Nadezhda, a school principal, whose small apartment already contained her own husband and daughter, her husband's sister, and Bulgakov's sister Vera; and Bulgakov's sister Yelena was on her way from Kiev. It was winter before Bulgakov and Lyubov found their own tiny apartment, where Bulgakov finished THE HEART OF A DOG and began adapting his half-published THE WHITE GUARD for the stage.

• • •

CHERUBIM: (Popping out from behind the curtain and applauding.) Production by Ametistov!
AMETISTOV: (Modestly) Oh, come on now...come on...

7. MOSCOW: THE MASTER AND THE MOSCOW ART THEATER

Boris Ilyich Vershilov was one of the people who read the sections of THE WHITE GUARD as they appeared in "Rossiya." Vershilov, a director on the staff of the Moscow Art Theater (MHAT), was impressed, and he recommended the work to Pavel Aleksandrovich Markov, the head of the MHAT literary department. The prestigious theater was in difficult, if not desperate, straits. Its famous actors were getting old, and it was coming to seem out-of-date, well past its days of glory. Konstantin Sergeyevich Stanislavsky and Vladimir Ivanovich Nemirovich-Danchenko, the founders and co-directors, were determined to bring the MHAT safely into the new era, but the only way of doing that was by finding strong new plays to revitalize it and restore its reputation. Markov thought THE WHITE GUARD might make just such a play, and he contacted Bulgakov in the spring of 1925 to propose a dramatization. He was surprised to find him already working on one.

On September 1, exceedingly nervous, chain-smoking and drinking a lot of water, Bulgakov read a draft of the new play to the MHAT company. By all accounts, it was a typically brilliant performance, the master storyteller knowing just how to bring all his characters to vivid life. The play was much praised, but everyone agreed it was much too long, and still too tied to the multitude of events and characters in the novel. With the unsolicited assistance of Markov and Ilya Sudakov, who would be the director, Bulgakov began another draft.

One of the pressures Bulgakov and his colleagues had to deal with as they tried to adapt THE WHITE GUARD for the stage was the fear of censorship and governmental interference. "Rossiya" had been banned, put out of business, before it could publish the final part of the novel, and new attacks on Bulgakov by important party hacks appeared regularly in the Soviet press. (Maxim Gorky, the most important and influential of post-Revolutionary writers, was a happy exception. Gorky admired and defended Bulgakov's work.)

The new draft, which Bulgakov read to the company in January 1926, was shorter and more focussed, and it had a working title, THE TURBIN FAMILY, without "White" in it, a much safer choice in the regime of the Reds. Rehearsals began, and the long rehearsal period was a time of more-than-usual tension. Bulgakov hated the impertinence of collective playwriting, just as Sudakov no doubt resented the group directing, with both Stanislavsky and Bulgakov leading rehearsals and giving notes to the actors. (Bulgakov, who thought little of Sudakov, was much praised by both Stanislavsky and the actors for his ability to discuss every role, even the smallest, in great detail. On the other hand, Bulgakov would sometimes discover Stanislavsky rehearsing scenes he hadn't written. The writer left a wickedly funny account of the frustrations of his early days at the MHAT in his THEATRICAL NOVEL.)

The political tensions reached a climax the day two investigators from the secret police arrived and searched Bulgakov's apartment. They were polite, but they frightened Bulgakov and Lyubov very much. They took away with them the only manuscript of Bulgakov's unpublished THE HEART OF A DOG (which he had recently agreed to adapt for the MHAT) and three notebooks that contained his 1921-26 diaries. Several months later, on the day of a dress rehearsal for THE DAYS

OF THE TURBINS (the title was finally chosen about that time), Bulgakov was taken to police headquarters and interrogated.

(The diaries were returned voluntarily in 1929, but Bulgakov feared they might still get him in trouble and destroyed them. He resolved never to keep a diary again and instead began sending autobiographical letters to a professor of philosophy who had expressed interest in writing his biography. Many of those letters have survived, but, so, miraculously, did the diaries. As it turned out, the police had made their own copies, which were unearthed and published in the Soviet Union in 1989-90. With Gorky's help, Bulgakov also got back THE HEART OF A DOG manuscript, two years after the confiscation.)

After all the pressures and the countless changes of the long and painful rehearsal process, THE DAYS OF THE TURBINS opened on October 5, 1926, in the midst of such tension that the theater asked Bulgakov not to sit in the audience on opening night. He watched from backstage, of course, but could not acknowledge the applause.

There was much to acknowledge. The audience was stunned, agitated, transported. The theater scholar Vitaly Vilenkin attended the second performance, at which Bulgakov was allowed to take a bow, and reported that the audience did not even get up during the intermissions. THE DAYS OF THE TURBINS was a sensation, just the new SEA GULL or THE LOWER DEPTHS that the troubled and drifting MHAT so badly needed, and, despite the controversy which continued to rage, it became one of the most popular and lucrative plays in the theater's history.

There was much criticism, from the left, of Bulgakov's sympathetic portrayal of a "White" family, but at least one Soviet critic confessed his surprise at being so moved by the plight of the "enemy." That the "Whites" were, after all, human beings was news to many: important news. The production seemed momentous, the harbinger of a new era of forgiveness and harmony. Many Russians came out of long emotional seclusion to weep for the Turbins, and for their own dead; to grieve openly for the world the war had swept away. As Ellendea Proffer writes, in her comprehensive, judicious, and illuminating BULGAKOV: LIFE AND WORK:

> It is hard for us now, whether we are Soviet or Western, to understand the shock of the first audiences at seeing this play. Here, after ten years of propaganda portrayals as "monsters of depravity," were live White Guardsmen, walking around a stage in those uniforms so weighted with emotional significance. Here was a vanished way of life, the passing of which was certainly regretted by part of the audience. The clothes and the table settings might have come from a hundred years before, so great were the changes since. The terrible year of 1918-1919 was back, on a stage, but there were viewers who forgot that it was all acting. At one performance a voice came from the audience at a tense moment: "Open the door! It's one of yours!"

The audiences may have loved THE DAYS OF THE TURBINS, but Bulgakov also kept track of his reviews, methodically pasting them in an album. He counted 301: 3 were positive, 298 negative. One, written by O. S. Litovsky and published in "Komsomol'skaya Pravda" ("Komsomol Truth"), reveals the true nature of Bulgakov's enemies:

> WHITE GUARD is the CHERRY ORCHARD of the White movement. What interest has the Soviet viewer in the suffering of landowner Ranevskaya, whose cherry orchard is mercilessly being cut down? What interest has the Soviet viewer in the sufferings of internal and external emigrés for their destroyed White movement? No interest at all. We don't need this.
>
> —Quoted in Proffer, BULGAKOV: LIFE AND WORK

The response of the audience, and the demand for tickets, were some consolation for such boorish attacks; and besides, Bulgakov had another play opening three weeks later.

• • •

AMETISTOV: (Looking over the apartment.) *Voilà*—It's paradise, isn't it, Count?

8. MOSCOW: *ZOYKA'S APARTMENT*

When the news got around that Bulgakov was writing a play for the MHAT, he received a visit from Aleksei Popov, the director of the Vakhtangov Theater. Popov wanted a new play, too.

The Vakhtangov Theater had been founded, as the Third Studio of the MHAT, by the young actor-director Evgeny Vakhtangov, who tried to steer a course between the very different systems of Moscow's two leading directors, Stanislavsky and Meyerhold. For Stanislavsky, the role of the actor was paramount. His method, a kind of psychological realism, attempted to bring a play to life by carefully recreating the physical and emotional life of each character. Meyerhold, the celebrated virtuoso of the avant-garde, focussed instead on the role of the inspired director. He used actors as puppets, often grotesque and exaggerated, in achieving the all-important spectacle. Playwrights occasionally failed to recognize their work in the hands of the great auteur.

In his production style, which was called "fantastic realism," Vakhtangov attempted to achieve a synthesis of those contrasting systems. He did not strive for a slavish imitation of life but for a kind of selective realism, with acting that might be expressionistic in style but would be psychologically true, as well. (Vakhtangov died in 1922, and the Third Studio was renamed for him.)

Bulgakov agreed to write a play for Popov and began to cast about for an idea. It is likely that he decided early on to write a play different in every way from THE DAYS OF THE TURBINS, a comedy that would explore the surprises, the mysteries, and the incongruities, of everyday life under the NEP. Many of his feuilletons and stories, as well as THE HEART OF A DOG, had been set in the context of the NEP wonderland, a subject, after all, that seems made for fantastic realism.

The idea of an NEP comedy was not new with Bulgakov. The moribund Russian theater had begun to revive with the economy, and a new theatrical genre had come into being to satirize the ubiquitous hustlers and corrupt officials of contemporary Moscow. Several such comedies had already appeared, including plays by writers (Romashov and Erdman, for example) who were friends of Bulgakov's. These satirical comedies have many similarities to ZOYKA'S APARTMENT in style, tone, plot, and characterization. Bulgakov was not so much an innovator of the new form as a perfector of it.

According to Lyubov's memoir, MY LIFE WITH MIKHAIL BULGAKOV, the primary source for her husband's NEP comedy was a story he came across in "The Red Gazette," an account of a police raid on a gambling den disguised as a dressmaker's shop in the apartment of a woman named Zoya Buyalskaya. In his excellent MIKHAIL BULGAKOV: A CRITICAL BIOGRAPHY, Lesley Milne reports being unable to locate that particular story in "The Red Gazette" or any other Russian newspaper of the time, but finding instead, from July to November 1925, accounts of the police discovering five secret brothels and seven opium dens. (Three of the opium dens had Chinese proprietors, and one had long operated behind the front of a Chinese laundry.) One inspector later recalled raiding a shady apartment belonging to one Zoya Shatova, who conducted a regular literary salon there.

Milne points out another intriguing real-life connection to ZOYKA. According to the memoirs of the writer V. Levshin, Gyorgy Yakulov, the celebrated set designer of the Kamerny Theater, actually lived in Pigit House, Zoya's building, and the sets S. Isakov created for ZOYKA'S APARTMENT were modelled on Yakulov's well-known studio. (Levshin says that Yakulov's place was always thereafter referred to as "Zoyka's apartment.")

As usual with Bulgakov, small details from his life or his earlier work slipped into the play. Abolyaninov has the playwright's previous addiction to morphine, Ametistov his passion for cards and gambling. An angel-faced Chinese killer with a Finnish knife and a longing for the hot sun, also called Tsen-Tsin-Poh (Cherubim's real name), had appeared in the author's "Chinese Story." Abolyaninov criticizes the color of the inspectors' shoes just as Lyubov teased him about his on the night they met. Bulgakov had been spending a lot of time at the 3-room apartment of his good friends the Komorskys (he conducted an unofficial Bulgakov salon there), and Zinaida Komorsky had a maid called "Manyushka." Bulgakov's Manyushka receives a polite but terrifying visit from the secret police, just as he and Lyubov had on the day his manuscripts were seized. Lyubov had an affected friend whom Bulgakov always referred to privately as "Mymra," a mildly derogatory nickname that means "Daffy" or "Dodo," and "Mymra" slipped into the play. And Lyubov, who had lived in Paris, may well have told her husband about buying dresses at Paquin's. Zoya orders her gowns from Paquin's, of course, and Ametistov claims to have worked there.

Bulgakov wrote ZOYKA'S APARTMENT toward the end of December 1925 and read it to the Vakhtangov company on January ll, 1926, four months after he had read his WHITE GUARD dramatization at the MHAT. Ruben Simonov, the actor Bulgakov chose to play Ametistov (the director had someone else in mind), said that Bulgakov read everything, "brilliantly," especially the role of Ametistov. The actors loved the play.

The rehearsals for ZOYKA'S APARTMENT were not as fraught with tension as those for THE DAYS OF THE TURBINS, but they were not without their difficulties. Popov and Bulgakov had some vigorous disagreements. More important, however, the moment for a playful, satirical glance at Russia under the NEP was quickly passing. Stalin, slowly seizing the reins of power, had begun eliminating his rivals. The urgency Zoya and her friends feel about acquiring rubles and getting out of the country mirrored a real desperation and fear on the streets and in the apartments of Moscow; and that made Bulgakov's comedy potentially dangerous, to the theater as well as to the playwright.

In fact, ZOYKA'S APARTMENT positively sparkled with dangerous elements: Ametistov's constant light-hearted mockery of the Party; Abolyaninov's description of the red-bearded thugs who threw him out of his apartment; Abolyaninov's description of the ridiculous genetic experiments of Soviet science; the playwright's portrayal of a new hierarchy in the classless society (the Very Important Woman), an absurd bureaucracy (Aliluya and his Apartment House Committee), a corrupt Soviet official (Goose), a comical secret police, and even (if the authorities could penetrate the heart of his mystery) a still militant, though admittedly anemic, White Russian Stiff.

The censors did not interfere with ZOYKA'S APARTMENT as intensely and repeatedly as they did with THE DAYS OF THE TURBINS, but they had their usual deleterious effect anyway, occasioning some level of self-censorship. The brief scene at "Headquarters" (Act III, scene 2), for example, was cut during rehearsals. We don't know why, but it seems likely that Bulgakov decided or was persuaded that it might be dangerous to include it.

More serious, perhaps, than what Bulgakov was prevailed upon to cut or soften was the pressure felt by the director to avert criticism by adopting a performance style that exaggerated the play's farcical elements. The make-up was stylized and grotesque, the set expressionistic. The actors were encouraged to indulge in broad, unrealistic, jokey business. Accounts of the production, as well as the tiresomely "funny" photographs that survive, suggest that Popov either did not realize, or did not dare to acknowledge, the real merit of the play.

Popov knew that ZOYKA'S APARTMENT would be attacked for lacking a clear didactic message. Bulgakov had not focused his satire at a specific, politically acceptable target, and he had not provided a model comrade to justify all the entertainingly bad behavior by making clear how it has been caused by reactionary attitudes, the tsarist past, etc. (In fact, Bulgakov mocks that very impulse, in the passage in which Aliluya tries to talk his way out of trouble with the inspectors:

Dear comrades, please take into consideration my humble beginnings in the ignorance and superstition that are the inescapable inheritance of the Tsarist times, and make your sentence conditional...what am I saying? I don't even understand it myself!)

Nevertheless, Popov found it expedient to claim some redeeming value for ZOYKA by passing it off as a sincere exposé of NEP crime and corruption. In a newspaper interview that appeared two days before the opening, Popov said he and the actors had had their doubts about the play during rehearsals, but had tried to insure its "ideological acceptability" by emphasizing its farcical nature and the depravity of its characters. "The tragedy is not that these characters suffer," he said, "...but that they have lost their humanity." To make Zoya less sympathetic, he made the unhappy actress (Tsetsiliya Mansurova) wear a false nose and a padded bottom. "*Adventurism, sordidness* and *depravity*: that is the fare of ZOYKA'S APARTMENT," he proclaimed. Popov may have fooled or mollified some of Bulgakov's critics, but he did so at the cost of infuriating the playwright.

ZOYKA'S APARTMENT opened on Oct 28, 1926, three weeks after the MHAT opened THE DAYS OF THE TURBINS. The critics dismissed the new comedy as a "a frankly frivolous entertainment for the philistine public" (or worse), but had generally high praise for the production and the acting, especially Isakov's expressionistic set, and the performances of Mansurova and Simonov as Zoya and Ametistov. Needless to say, the philistine public loved it.

• • •

AMETISTOV: ...But where are we going? Tell me, dear comrade, where shall we go? Oh, my star, my restless and wandering star!...Oh, my destiny!...

9. MOSCOW: A SOVIET DESTINY

Like THE DAYS OF THE TURBINS, ZOYKA'S APARTMENT was a tremendous hit. Critics sniffed that the bourgeoisie went to the former in order to cry and the latter in order to laugh. Stalin was apparently philistine enough to enjoy both plays. He attended fifteen performances of DAYS, eight of ZOYKA. Both DAYS and ZOYKA were still going strong when a third Bulgakov play, THE

CRIMSON ISLAND, opened at the Kamerny Theater in December 1928. A fourth play, FLIGHT, was ready to go into rehearsal at the MHAT whenever the censors passed it, and the MHAT had also commissioned an adaptation of THE HEART OF A DOG. Even Meyerhold asked Bulgakov for a play. (Bulgakov said no.)

The fall from such glory was swift. In response to the long critical campaign against the writer, and the strong pressure of recent attacks in the press, the Central Repertory Committee of the People's Commissariat of Education banned FLIGHT in October 1928 (Stalin called the play "an anti-Soviet phenomenon"), and ZOYKA'S APARTMENT was pulled from the repertory in December.

1929 would be a difficult year for Russia, as the NEP gave way to the first Five-Year-Plan and Stalin's purges and show trials began. By March THE DAYS OF THE TURBINS and THE CRIMSON ISLAND had been banned. Though the MHAT was allowed to revive DAYS in 1932, and though Bulgakov had other plays passed for production before being finally banned, he never had another new play produced or book published as long as he lived.

Cut off at the height both of his creative power and his popular success, unable to support himself by writing and in worsening financial circumstances, Bulgakov's increasing frustration and despair led him to take a bold, even perhaps foolhardy, step. He sent Stalin a letter, requesting to be allowed either to work or to leave the country. Against all expectations, Stalin got in touch with him by telephone and, in a fraught and elliptical conversation, suggested that he apply again for a job at the MHAT. (The dictator may have been eager to prevent the propaganda setback of another leading Soviet writer committing suicide: the popular Futurist poet and playwright Vladimir Mayakovsky had killed himself four days before the surprising phone call.) Bulgakov did as Stalin suggested, and he was promptly engaged, first as a literary consultant to the propagandistic Theater of Proletarian Youth (a job he despised) and then as an assistant director at the MHAT.

At the end of February 1929, Bulgakov met a woman named Yelena Sergeyevna Shilovskaya, the courageous, sophisticated, playful wife of a Soviet lieutenant-general with whom she had two sons. She shared Bulgakov's world and interests even more fully than Lyubov did. Yelena had thought of becoming an actress, and had translated plays by the French writers André Maurois and Jean Giraudoux. Her sister was Nemirovich-Danchenko's secretary and the wife of an actor who had played in THE DAYS OF THE TURBINS. Yelena became good friends with the Bulgakovs. She was increasingly devoted to the writer and his work. When he began composing THE CABAL OF HYPOCRITES, a play about Molière's difficulties with *his* autocrat, he was dictating it to both Lyubov and Yelena, but only Yelena could type.

In February 1931, unwilling to tear apart two families, Yelena and Bulgakov decided to separate; but a year and a half later, in August 1932, Yelena sent word asking to see him. When they met, they realized they were still in love. They quickly secured their divorces and were married on Oct 4.

Yelena Bulgakova nurtured and cared for her husband, the man and the writer, devotedly, until his early death. Among other things, she inspired and encouraged the despairing and ailing writer to finish his masterpiece, THE MASTER AND MARGARITA, and then, for many long years after his death, she preserved in secret the precious manuscript. Bulgakov died at his home on March 10, 1940, at the same age (48) and of the same disease (sclerosis of the kidneys) that killed his father. It would be many years before his unfortunate countrymen could read his novels, and see his plays on their stages, and learn how uncommonly alive he remains.

• • •

ABOLYANINOV: That's because this regime has made it impossible for decent people to survive.
AMETISTOV: *Pardon, pardon!* Decent people can survive anything. I'm a decent person, and I'm surviving...

10. EPILOGUE: "WHAT WILL BECOME OF US?"

Bulgakov returned to ZOYKA'S APARTMENT in 1934-35, when the prospect of a production at the Vieux Colombier Theater in Paris caused him to hope for a Russian revival. The world had changed a lot since 1926, the year the play opened. The Roaring Twenties had given way to the Grim Thirties, and all sorts of excitements, permissions, and possibilities had vanished with the NEP. Many of the elements in the 1926 text were no longer appropriate, or permissible, or safe. Besides, Bulgakov had since written THE CABAL OF HYPOCRITES, an unproduced and unpublished masterpiece about another playwright willing to butcher his masterpiece in the hope of getting it approved for performance under a different autocrat.

The French production of ZOYKA'S APARTMENT caused the playwright a great deal of anxiety. He learned that the translator-adaptors, Marie Reinhardt and Benjamin Crémieux, had turned Goos into a Jew and were adding lines critical of the Soviet Union. This could be very dangerous for him, of course, so he called on his brother Nikolai to intervene. The production, which opened in February 1937 without the "improvements," was a mild success.

Meanwhile, dreaming of seeing ZOYKA on stage again in Russia, Bulgakov revised it extensively, changing (by Proffer's estimate) more than 40 per cent of the text. The 1926 text, written in five days, is by general agreement the less polished and shapely version. On the other hand, in the 1935 text the playwright has not only cut and rewritten passages to prune dialogue that is too long or not strong enough, he has also lost or weakened some good speeches, obscured important details, and sacrificed wonderful material that is too risqué for the Thirties or too satirical for the unreliable sense of humor of the older Stalin.

Zoya's paintings are gone in the 1935 text, both the nude that Goos admires and the portrait of Karl Marx it has replaced. The workshop scene has been cut altogether, and the atelier scene has been shortened. Lizanka doesn't expire "crucified by cocaine on the cold boulevards of Moscow" and Madame Ivanova no longer offers to show Goos her slashes nor sits on his lap. The party scene has been substantially curtailed. Lizanka's kiss is no longer auctioned. The disappointed homosexual Smoker who won it is gone, as are the Poet and the Foxtrotter. The Stiff (or Dead Body of Ivan Vassilyevich) is neither anemic (drained of blood?), nor from Rostov-on-the-Don, and he no longer launches into rousing anti-Communist or Cossack songs or threatens to string people up when his men arrive. 1935 was not the time to be playing around, however elliptically, with the restless, howling ghost of White Russia.

Zoya's exchange with Aliluya about being socially dangerous "only to those who are socially dangerous to me" is gone in the revised text, and Aliluya's name has become Portupeya. (Proffer speculates ingeniously that "Aliluya" may have been too close to "Alliluyeva," the name of Stalin's wife.) Goos has had a name change, too. In 1926 he is Goos-Remontny, "reconditioned goose," a reference both to his new status as an important Soviet official and to the bizarre genetic experiments that were a feature of early Soviet science (c.f. Abolyaninov's story of the "nasty experiment" that has turned a chicken into a rooster). In 1935 he has become Goos-Bagazhny, "goose of the baggage," a softer image, perhaps a reference to how much power he carries or how many rubles he has managed to pack away. There is no allusion in 1935 to Lunacharsky's beard or to the powerful People's Commissariat of Education, and Ametistov no longer mentions selling the stolen postcard portraits of "our beloved leaders." There is less talk of escaping to Paris, and less nostalgia for the good old days.

The existence of these two texts, with different virtues and different flaws, creates both a great problem and an opportunity for translators. We cannot be certain how Bulgakov would have revised ZOYKA'S APARTMENT in 1935 if he had had no fear of Stalin and his censors. We can't even be sure what form the 1926 text would take, if the playwright had then been free to write, and the Vakhatangov to perform, without fear.

This translation of ZOYKA'S APARTMENT, a revised and expanded version of one previously published by the present translators, is an adaptation by those who don't generally believe in adaptations. In this case, however, a higher kind of fidelity to the play and playwright seemed to require some attempt to preserve the best elements of both Russian texts. We have tried, therefore, to achieve a faithful translation of a non-existent text, the text Bulgakov himself would have written if he had been free to write whatever he pleased. We have not subjected the play to false improvements by substituting our own lines, or jokes, or topical references, and we have not invented lines, nor rearranged the order of his, unless it has been necessary to do so, as unobtrusively as possible, in order to make seamless our joining of material from the different texts.

ZOYKA'S APARTMENT is the story of a complex post-Revolutionary heroine, Zoya Denisovna Peltz, who seizes her NEP opportunity by exploiting her only asset, a large apartment in a rapidly-expanding city with an acute housing shortage, in order to escape, with her helpless, aristocratic lover, from their perilous homeland. In reinventing herself as an entrepreneur, Zoya reluctantly turns for assistance to an ambiguous old friend, Aleksander Tarasovich Ametistov. In the time since she's seen him, Ametistov has become just what she needs, an expert at survival. The necessary man, the "accomplished rascal" sufficient unto the day, Ametistov has been preparing to be a Nepman all his life.

The play is also the story of the apartment itself, and of the ordinary-extraordinary men and women, a wide cross-section of the community, who pass through it. They are exotic but believable creatures, more sinned against than sinning, the descendants of those same Russians who wrestled for so many slow decades with the great philosophical question, "What is to be done?" Lenin and the Bolsheviks had decisively answered that question for the foreseeable future, but another had arisen in the hearts of the Russian people: not "What is to be done?" but "What will become of me?"

It's a smaller, less heroic question, but the world they live in has less scope for heroism, and they have to spend most of their time and energy just trying to stay alive. Zoya, Ametistov, Abolyaninov, Aliluya, Goose, the women in the workshop, the models, the guests at the party: they're all ridiculous, of course, but as we discover their various defects, we also learn what makes them human—their pretensions, their disappointments, their hopes and dreams—and we warm to them. Even Cherubim's murder of Goose, seen in the context of his painful yearning to get back to "warm Shanghai," does not put him beyond the reach of our sympathy. Bulgakov's art is brisk and witty, but it is also generous, tender, compassionate. The reason the first audiences responded so enthusiastically to ZOYKA'S APARTMENT is that they saw themselves on the Vakhtangov stage, insufficiently disguised by the grotesque make-up, brave and frightened little people trying to survive as they rode the whirlwind under their own restless and wandering stars. If we look closely, we can recognize these characters, too. We grow to care what will become of them because we know them so well; and that compromised, complicated world in which they dream and struggle—that's our world, too.

The Translators

ZOYKA'S APARTMENT, Mikhail Bulgakov's tragic farce, is the fourth Russian classic to be translated by Nicholas Saunders and Frank Dwyer and published by Smith and Kraus, Inc. It is a revised and expanded version of the translation/adaptation originally commissioned by Circle in the Square (NYC), produced in the 1989-90 Broadway season under the title ZOYA'S APARTMENT, and subsequently published by Samuel French, Inc. In the spring of 1996, Mr. Dwyer will direct a reading of the new text at the Mark Taper Forum, in Los Angeles, where he serves as Literary Manager.

The first Saunders-Dwyer translation, Anton Chekhov's early romantic comedy, THE WOOD DEMON, had its highly-acclaimed premiere, under Mr. Dwyer's direction, on the Taper mainstage in the spring of 1994 in a production that marked the debut of the L.A. classical ensemble, the Antaeus Company. A new translation of a second Chekhov play, THE SEA GULL, was commissioned by Timothy Near, Artistic Director of the San Jose Repertory Theatre, and premiered there under her direction, also with great success, just as THE WOOD DEMON ended its run in Los Angeles. The translators turned next to THE SUMMER PEOPLE, Maxim Gorky's still urgent, moving depiction of a whole community in political and moral crisis. THE SUMMER PEOPLE was given a reading, directed by Mr. Dwyer and with Mr. Saunders in the role of Kolon, in the 1994-95 Taper New Work Festival. For their next project, the collaborators have returned to Chekhov; they are currently at work on a new translation of THE CHERRY ORCHARD.

In a distinguished career as actor and director, Mr. Saunders has appeared in 19 Broadway shows and hundreds of television programs, but is perhaps best remembered as Captain Barker in the old Phil Silvers "Sergeant Bilko" series. He played the role of Chubukov in the 1990 premiere of his own translation of Chekhov's THE MARRIAGE PROPOSAL. He is a member of the Antaeus Company and played the role of Orlovsky ("Godfather") in the Taper premiere of THE WOOD DEMON. A native Russian, Mr. Saunders has had a parallel career in the Russian language field, rising to be Production and Presentation Manager of the Russian Department at Radio Liberty. He proudly claims four generations of actors in his happy family.

Mr. Dwyer, formerly a member of the Repertory Theater of Lincoln Center and CSC Repertory Theater, is a founding member of the Antaeus Company in Los Angeles. He was seen at the Mark Taper Forum in the Antaeus workshop of the Feydeau-Desvallières farce, LES FIANCÉS DE LOCHES, translated as A FLAW IN THE OINTMENT by Lillian Garrett-Groag and William Gray. As an actor, Mr. Dwyer has appeared on Broadway, and at such theaters as the New York Shakespeare Festival, Playwrights Horizons, Roundabout, and the Quaigh, where he played the title role in the New York premiere of Slavomir Mrozek's VATZLAV. His recent performance as Falstaff in an adaptation of both parts of Shakespeare's HENRY IV at the Odyssey Theater was lauded by LA critics. Mr. Dwyer was founding Artistic Director of the short-lived Yankee Repertory Theater in New York City, for which he directed a revival of THE FIREBUGS, by Max Frisch. A prizewinning poet, he has also written young adult biographies of DANTON, KING HENRY VIII, KING JAMES I, and JOHN ADAMS. He is married to actress-writer Mary Stark.